The House of Quality in a Minute

A Guide to Quality Function Deployment (3rd Ed.)

The House of Quality in a Minute

A Guide to Quality Function Deployment (3rd Ed.)

by

Christian N. Madu
*Pace University, United States
and University of Nigeria, Nsukka*

INFORMATION AGE PUBLISHING, INC.
Charlotte, NC • www.infoagepub.com

Library of Congress Cataloging-in-Publication Data

CIP record for this book is available from the Library of Congress
http://www.loc.gov

ISBNs: 978-1-64113-903-8 (Paperback)

978-1-64113-904-5 (Hardcover)

978-1-64113-905-2 (ebook)

CONTENTS

PREFACE

The House of Quality (QFD) in a Minute is written with two primary objectives. First, to introduce the reader to the basics of quality function deployment (QFD) which is a quality tool that is widely used in corporations and second, to prepare practitioners to understand and use the concepts of QFD without costly training and seminars on the basics of QFD. With knowledgeof the basics, advanced training becomes more effective.

This book demonstrates in a simple form how other techniques such as the analytic hierarchy process (AHP) can be used effectively in QFD charts. It helps decision makers to make consistent decisions which would help to ensure that appropriate customer requirements are matched with the right design requirements. It is also important to understand the role of QFD within the overall quality imperative of a firm. Thus, the book demonstrates the linkages between QFD and other important quality programs such as quality control charts, benchmarking, and concurrent engineering.

QFD is part of an organization's strategy. The need to integrate QFD within the firm's strategic plan is demonstrated in this book. The driving force behind the use of QFD is to help the firm to design products and services that satisfy customer requirements by listening to the voice of the customer. It is shown in this book that a firm can improve on its productivity, control costs, increase market share, and remain competitive through the application of QFD.

Like the previous editions, this edition is written with the reader in mind to provide a simple and quick understanding of this important technique. The book has also been expanded to include new chapters on identifying customer needs and process change management initiatives. The book can be used as a quick reference guide by anyone involved in quality management and deployment. Consultants, managers, practitioners, and engineers in both the public and private sectors irrespective of whether they are involved in manufacturing or service operations, will find this book very useful. Students and instructors of quality management will also continue to find this book very useful.

Like the previous editions, short cases and test questions are provided at the end of each chapter. This book is the right place to start the journey to understanding QFD. It is basic but direct to the point. It is very precise and in fact, many Japanese managers resort to basic books such as this to understand the emerging management tools and techniques that help them to become competitive. Finally, I extend my thanks to all those who have provided me feedback on how to improve the book, and readers worldwide who made the 1st and 2nd editions a great success. I especially thank my many students over the years who have made inputs in my work. Your commitment and support have always been inspirational in developing new projects. I also thank my family for all the support they have given me in support of this project.

My research work and activities continue to benefit from the generosity of The Shell Petroleum Development Company of Nigeria Limited (SPDC) who endowed me with the SPDC JV Professorship in Environmental Management & Control at the University of Nigeria. The resources provided by the position continue to make it possible for me to expand my research scope in and beyond the areas of environmental management.

Christian N. Madu
Pace University New York, NY

CHAPTER 1

HISTORY AND DEFINITION OF QUALITY FUNCTION DEPLOYMENT (QFD)

The American Supplier Institute (1989) defines Quality Function Deployment (QFD), as "a system for translating consumer requirements into appropriate company requirements at each stage from research and development to engineering and manufacturing to marketing/sales and distribution." Simply, QFD involves listening to the "voice of the customer" and systematically, translating the customer's requirements through each phase of the product development stage as requirements that the product must meet. It shifts away emphasis from meeting management and engineering demands in product development to that of meeting customers' demands. Customer requirements are translated into requirements that must be met to deliver quality product or service to the customer. Listening to the "voice of the customer" starts from the product development stage and it is deployed throughout the firm. The focus of QFD is to maximize resources and minimize waste. QFD is therefore, a planning tool for developing new products and improving existing products (Vonderembse & Van Fossen, 1998). Other definitions of QFD are offered as follows: Akao (1990) defined QFD as "a method for developing a design quality aimed at satisfying the consumer and then translating the consumer's demand into

The House of Quality in a Minute:
A Guide to Quality Function Deployment (3rd Ed.), pp. 1–7

design targets and major quality assurance points to be used throughout the production phase." Thus, QFD assures that quality is designed into the product. By doing this, a considerable reduction in product development time is achieved. Sullivan (1986) defined QFD as "The main objective of any manufacturing company to bring new (and carryover) products to market sooner than the competition with lower cost and improved quality." He went on to emphasize that this concept involves the translation of customer requirements to appropriate technical requirements for each stage of the product development and production. This process involves the marketing strategies, planning, product design and engineering, prototype evaluation, production process development, production and sales. Apparent from this definition is the fact that QFD applies also to existing products and services. Furthermore, QFD involves the entire product life cycle as well as the entire functional units of a business process. It leads to designing quality into the product by designing customer requirements into the product. More importantly, it significantly leads to a reduction in product development and early introduction of the product to the marketplace. Another objective of QFD is the optimal utilization of resources by ensuring that the product demanded by customers is produced correctly the first time and ensuring its introduction on a timely fashion.

QFD offers new challenges to businesses. It involves the entire "value supply chain" of the organization. It is important to evaluate each product development stage to see how it aligns with customer's requirements and the resources of the firm. This will therefore, lead to new set of standards and targets not only for engineers involved with product design but also to production workers at the floor level and suppliers. Thus, the entire supply chain is influenced by the "voice of the customer" (Day, 1993; Evans & Lindsay, 1999; Gale & Wood, 1994).

Clearly, listening to the "voice of the customer" and translating customer requirements into achievable targets to improve product quality is not easy. There will be some conflicting requirements. The customer may identify requirements that are not attainable at the same level, for example, the need to manufacture the best copy paper and also, protect the environment. These two are contradictory since the "best quality copy paper" will rely on 100% virgin pulp which may conflict with the desire to protect the forestry. However, a copy paper that uses a mixture of virgin pulp and recycled pulp could be produced to balance this tradeoff. QFD, attempts to resolve such conflicts by focusing on the most important requirements. Furthermore, customer needs must be balanced with design requirements and specifications. Some of the customer needs may not be attainable or feasible due to limitations in technology or available resources. Thus, customer needs, which are often referred to, as "whats" should be balanced with design requirements, referred to as "hows." The translation of "whats" into "hows" could be difficult and complex, as the "hows" may be interdependent and/ or, negatively correlated to each other. This may present another source of conflict that may also need to be resolved.

We have focused to this point on meeting customer requirements through QFD. There are many ways to solicit customer requirements. Notably, these requirements could be gathered through various market research methods such as customer survey questionnaires, interviews, focus groups, telephone surveys. A list of customer requirements is generated through this process and is referred to as "spoken" quality demands and performance expectations. However, there may be some product attributes that are assumed by the customer or the customer may not be aware of but may add to the value of the product. Such attributes should also be included and are referred to as "unspoken" attributes. Thus, the aim is not just to meet the requirements as specified or identified by the customer but also to go beyond and add as much features as possible and feasible to make the product the best in its class.

BRIEF HISTORY OF QFD

The origins of QFD can be traced to Mitsubishi's Heavy Industries Kobe shipyard in Japan in late 1960s where QFD was used to facilitate cross-functional product development process (Eseteghalian, Verma, Foutz, & Thompson, 1998). A 1986 survey by the Japanese Union of Scientists and Engineers (JUSE) showed that more than half of the companies surveyed was using QFD. The application of QFD is pervasive in many of the manufacturing and service sectors in Japan. Toyota Motor Company and its suppliers are also among the major companies that have applied QFD in Japan. It is reported that Toyota auto body achieved a 60% reduction in start-up costs for its new car model launch as a result of QFD application. Although pre-production cost went up slightly, other major costs were slashed by about 80%. Manufacturers from the United States were, however, slow in applying QFD. Its first major applications were in the automotive and electronic industries.

QFD is known by several names. As Emmanuel and Kroll (1998) note, the original name for QFD in Japan is *hin shitsu, ki nou, ten kai*. There are several translations for these words including "features mechanization evolution, qualities function diffusion, or quality function deployment." The problem here is in the direct translation of the original Japanese words to English language. Other popular names used for QFD include Policy Deployment, Voice of the Customer, House of Quality, Customer-Driven Engineering, and Matrix Product Planning.

MOTIVATION FOR QFD

Undoubtedly, the increased competition in both the United States and global markets helped to focus the attention of U.S. businesses on the application of QFD. As Emmanuel and Kroll (1998) note, the QFD as a planning tool, reached the U.S. during the quality revolution of the 1980s. Japanese companies were gradually taking over many of the businesses that U.S. manufacturers once dominated. There was a significant interest by top management to understand Japanese management practices especially as they relate to product quality. Major companies in the U.S. embarked on studying these new quality philosophies that were coming out from Japan. Furthermore, they understood that in order to compete effectively, they must realign their strategies and develop plans like their Japanese counterparts that focus on achieving customer satisfaction. QFD became one of the important tools that could help them understand the customer and integrate the customer's requirements into the design and production of goods and services. By doing so, they will be able to regain lost markets and compete effectively. The incentive for survival in today's business was therefore, a motivating force in the adoption of these new practices by American businesses.

Hales and David (1995) note that product failures could be devastating to a company and may drain both the human and financial resources. They point out that some companies that maintain volumes of information pertaining to the customer and state-of-the art design and manufacturing tools have witnessed high-profile flops. For example, products such as new Coke, dry beer, and smokeless cigarettes. Therefore, the emphasis with QFD is not merely to collect volumes of information on customer requirements but to be able to develop a structured and systematic approach when analyzing such information and translate its results to the design and manufacture of customer-driven products. They note that sometimes, products or services that customers do not want manifest themselves in terms of "functionality, practicality, quality, cost, timing" and so forth. They advocate the use of QFD with target costing to get a company to be customer-focused. QFD emphasizes the fact that the product can be designed and produced to meet the customer requirements. However, cost should be a consideration in determining what the market could bear.

BENEFITS OF QFD

QFD has many demonstrable benefits especially for firms interested in achieving competitiveness, increasing market share, improving productivity and improving the bottom line. Those companies that have adopted QFD have reported significant cost reductions. How these gains are achieved are outlined below:

- Reduction in cycle time is achieved. The product is introduced to the market faster. Start-up costs are lower. Quality is improved. There is a reduction in number of engineering changes that may be required.
- Products are produced at a lower cost due to the reduction in operational cost.
- QFD is normally applied in a cross-functional team context. For example, members from the different functional areas of the firm organize to develop new product concepts. Members of the cross-functional team have diverse backgrounds and can share common information and understand each other's views. This process of sharing information and listening to each other, helps resolve potential conflicts and assures that organizational goals are not suboptimized. Members begin to develop a more holistic picture of the problem. Information gathered from the different functional teams can also be shared. For example, marketing, sales, and distribution departments often have more contact with customers. They can relay information obtained through this process to those in engineering who will have to incorporate such considerations during product design and development.
- Information gathering is an ongoing process in the use of QFD. It is important to maintain a database of customer requirements that may be gathered from different sources. This information could be used repeatedly to design new product or improve existing products.
- Design and production efficiency is achieved through QFD. Members of the cross-functional teams develop a critical analysis of their functions and ensure that customer requirements are integrated at every phase of product development. This will ensure that the products are designed and produced right the first time. Thus, reducing the cost of production, minimizing waste, and maximizing efficiency.
- Organizational harmony may foster through formation of cross-functional teams. The functional units will no longer be competing against each other rather, they will be working towards a common goal. Such teams foster increased openness and sharing of information with the ultimate goal of designing and producing products that will lead to high customer satisfaction.

- Problems are easier to identify by listening to the "voice of the customer." These problems can be corrected to achieve successful introduction of the product in the marketplace. Also, a decision-making process may include significant customer groups in the team to help ensure that the products are designed and produced with the customer in mind.
- Market information gained through QFD can be used to determine product price, quality, and functionality.
- Product development is customer-driven and supports value-engineering analysis in order to cut cost and add value to the product.
- Bottom line is improved through the application of QFD. Some of the reported influence on bottom line are as follows:

  o   High market acceptance of the product
  o   Reduction in design cycle time
  o   Increased competitiveness
  o   Reduction in design changes
  o   Reduction in production cost
  o   Improved efficiency.
  o   Improved worker morale.

Bagel Sales Double at Host Marriot

Host Marriot used QFD to improve quality and customer satisfaction. Host Marriot controls more than 70% of the food and beverage sales in US airports and it is the leading provider of food and beverages to the traveling public.

It needed a new approach to address the three trends in how travelers view airport food: (1) Healthier and lighter food, (2) more female travelers, and (3) serving of fewer on-board meals. To change from its traditional approach that was profit-driven to new product and service development that will focus on customer satisfaction, Host Marriot employed QFD. QFD is used to emphasize the importance of quality and customer satisfaction. This led to dramatic increases in sales (Lampa & Glenn, 1996).

CONCLUSION

In summary, QFD is a planning tool that can help businesses plan product design and production with increased efficiency. Its aim is to ensure that customer requirements are integrated in the design and production of the product. By doing so, a product that meets high quality standards as defined by the customer can be produced. This ensures that the product is not offered to the customer as seen by the design engineer but rather as seen by the customer itself. If the customer's requirements are effectively considered, then it is likely that the customer will accept the final product. This will help improve the competitiveness of the manufacturer, ensure customer loyalty, reduce waste, and improve the bottom line. The next chapter will focus on the "voice of the customer" (Akao, 1990).

SELF STUDY QUESTIONS

1. QFD involves listening to the _____and translating the customer's requirements through each phase of the product development stage.
2. What are the spoken and unspoken quality demands and performance expectations? What is the role of QFD in this regard?
3. In order for QFD to be customer focused it should be used in combination with which method of costing? Mention three benefits of QFD.

REFERENCES

Akao, Y. (1990). *Quality function deployment.* Cambridge, MA: Productivity Press.

American Supplier Institute. (1989). *Quality function deployment implementation manual.* Dearborn, MI: American Supplier Institute.

Day, R. G. (1993). *Quality function deployment—Linking a company with its customers.* Milwaukee, WI: ASQC Quality Press.

Emmanuel, J. T., & Kroll, D. E. (1998). Concurrent engineering. In D. N. Madu (Ed.), *Handbook of total quality management.* Boston, MA: Kluwer.

Eseteghalian, A., Verma, B., Foutz, T., & Thompson, S. (1998). Customer focused approach to design: new methodologies consider environmental impact on product development. *Engineering & Technology for a Sustainable World,* 7(2). Pages?

Evans, J. R., & Lindsay, W. M. (1999). *The management & control of quality* (4th ed.) Cincinnati, OH: South-Western.

Gale, B. T., & Wood, R. C. (1994). Managing customer value-creating quality and service that customers can see. New York, NY: The Free Press.

Hales, R., & Staley, D. (1995, Jan. 2). Mix target costing, QFD for successful new products. *Marketing News,* 22(1), 18–20.

Lampa, S., & Glenn M. (1996). *Bagel sales double at Host Marriot.* The Eighth Symposium on Quality Function Deployment. Retrieved from http://www.mazur.net/works/bagel_qfd_at_host_7qfds.pdf

Mears, P. (1995). *Quality improvement tools & techniques.* New York, NY: McGraw Hill.

Sullivan, L. P. (1986, June). Quality function deployment. *Quality Progress, 19,* 39–50.

Vonderembse, M. A., & Van Fossen, T. (1998). Quality Function Deployment. In C. N. Madu (Ed.), *Handbook of total quality management.* Boston, MA: Kluwer.

CHAPTER 2

VOICE OF THE CUSTOMER

Quality function deployment (QFD) is a process of listening to the "voice of the customer," identifying the customer's needs, and incorporating those needs in the design and production of goods and services. We noted in Chapter 1 that this process involves the entire supply chain with the goal of producing the goods or services that the customer actually wants and adding value to those goods and services. Listening to the "voice of the customer" ensures the manufacturer or service provider that features the customer wants are included in the product or service. The key fact, however, is listening to the "voice of the customer" and identifying customer requirements as articulated by the customer. The aim of this chapter is to specifically outline how manufacturers can make effective use of this learning process.

There are three levels in listening to the "voice of the customer." The first level involves an understanding of the basic wants and needs of the customer. This involves the use of experimental techniques to identify customer requirements. Experimental approaches to be taken here include the use of field surveys, focus groups, questionnaires, to identify a list of requirements that are "important" to the customer. These requirements must be translated into measurable operational forms. For example, a homeowner's requirement to a builder that the house be well built is vague and does not identify what features will make the house well built. Therefore, the request needs to be broken down to specific points such

The House of Quality in a Minute:
A Guide to Quality Function Deployment (3rd Ed.), pp. 9–17
Copyright © 2020 by Information Age Publishing

as: the foundation should be supported by adequate pillars, the electric outlets work, the trims are in place, the doors close properly, the walls are smooth, the ceilings are high, and so forth. In other words, vague statements by customers must be broken down to operational forms. These as we stated earlier are the "spoken" quality attributes that must be present in the home. However, there are other "unspoken" attributes that the builder must include. For example, what effect will extreme weather conditions have on the house? Is the house accident proof? Thus, both the "spoken" and "unspoken" customer requirements must be present if the "voice of the customer" is to be heard.

The second phase involves the extension of the product design beyond these "spoken" and "unspoken" customer requirements. There are some customers' requirements that are not apparent from the first phase that designers should be aware of. Designers need to scrutinize how and why customers use their product (Vonderembse & Van Fossen, 1998). Alternative ways should be offered to cover this range of applications and usage by customers. For example, consider a college in a metropolitan area that attracts adult students. These students may be primarily interested in quality education but may also be interested in the convenience of getting higher education. There is a variety of ways that the college could provide this service to its student population. One way may be to offer evening programs. Another way may be to offer weekend classes. Other more technologically advanced forms may be to offer lectures through videoconferencing at their job sites, or online classes. By doing this, QFD drives the company by forcing the design team to identify hidden customer requirements and offering ways to satisfy such requirements.

Third, there are many features of the product that the customer may be unaware of. However, the cross-functional team that works on the QFD can identify these features and point them out to the customer. Customers are often unaware of advances in technology and research that could help improve the quality of the product. For example, with the growing focus on sustainable development, a manufacturer may identify new ways to minimize waste or use less energy in product design and production. This may increase customer satisfaction and help the manufacturer expand its market share. The manufacturer could increase customer satisfaction by trying to understand the customer beyond the horizon of the product and determining what is important to the customer. It is important to understand the customer's behavior and how that may affect some of his actions. For example, a customer interested in buying a new car, may identify operational features such as aesthetics, dependability, and availability of service as features of interest to her. However, the same customer may be interested in cars that burn cleaner and consume less gas. Safety issues may also be important, and the customer may prefer cars that offer a combination of product features as well as these other important attributes.

FORMATION OF CROSS-FUNCTIONAL TEAMS

Cross-functional teams are used in most QFD projects. The team will comprise of representatives from the different functional departments or units that are either directly or indirectly affected by the project. In a business organization, this team could include representatives from engineering, marketing, production, and finance. The objective or the goal of the team will be to find an efficient method to address customer needs or requirements in the design, production, and delivery of products and services. Thus, this team must address the feasibility of using the organization's resources to satisfy customer requirements. The use of cross-functional teams also has other important benefits to the organization as follows:

- It ensures that all the related functional units are committed to the project. When members of these teams participate in the project, they are committed to the successful completion of the project.
- Organizations use their resources more efficiently if the various functional units work towards a common goal. The use of cross-functional teams exposes members of the team to the need for achieving organizational goals and helps reduce internal competition. Therefore, marketing will not see its goals as different from that of engineering. The different units will come to understand the purpose of the organization as that of satisfying customer requirements in a more efficient way. And, once that is achieved, customer satisfaction will also be attained and the business will thrive.
- The use of teams enables information sharing. For example, product designers come to learn from marketing how the customer perceives certain aspects of the product. Designers come to learn from finance about the financial viability or feasibility of certain projects. Through teams, information flows laterally and can be used timely for effective decision making.
- Customers are the major beneficiaries of cross-functional team activities. The different functional groups have different worldviews, which helps broaden each participant's scope and view. These different perspectives could be instrumental in designing products that appeal to a wider range of consumer groups.
- Members in cross-functional teams are empowered. They feel the responsibility to make decisions and take corrective actions.

This will also increase their organizational commitment and helps reduce organizational waste. Morale and motivation may also improve.

- Through cross-functional teams, brainstorming sessions can be held to generate ideas for product improvement and development.

Although cross-functional teams are heralded as useful in designing and producing high quality products, however, such teams could become counterproductive if not well implemented. Some of the problems that may arise are as follows:

- Group-think mentality can often emerge from any team. This happens when members perceive domination of the team by one or few individuals. So, rather than team members actively participating and contributing their ideas, they become subjected to accept the views of one or more dominant members of the group. This must be avoided if customer requirements are to be satisfied.
- Feeling of alienation may emerge. This again, is related to the group-think mentality. This happens when members feel that they have no role to play other than to rubber stamp preconceived ideas.
- Conflicts may often arise. However, it is important to productively resolve any conflicts and avoid formation of interest groups within the cross-functional groups. Formation of conflicting subgroups will invariably lead to suboptimization.

It is important for members of cross-functional teams to have an open mind about the problem to be solved and work towards a common goal— that of the organization's success by improving customer satisfaction. This can be achieved by focusing on what is important to the customer and how the organization can satisfy the customer using its resources.

IDENTIFYING CUSTOMER REQUIREMENTS

The entire premise of QFD rests on identifying and satisfying customer requirements. Although many QFD research have presented examples of customer requirements and how they have been matched with design requirements, few have really discussed in detail how customer requirements are identified. Granted, many have mentioned techniques such as the use of focus groups, marketing information, and so forth, it is important to have a systematic way to identify customer requirements. Customer requirements form the foundation of QFD. If the wrong requirements are identified, the product designed to meet such requirements will lose its appeal and will therefore, fail. The "identification of customer requirements" is the most critical step in developing a QFD. We shall examine two popular methods to identify customer requirements. These methods focus mostly on identifying the "spoken requirements" of the customer. Hayes (1992) refers to the first method as "quality dimension development approach." The second method was developed by Flanagan (1954) and it is known as the "critical incident approach." Further discussions on identifying customer needs will be provided in Chapter 3.

QUALITY DIMENSION DEVELOPMENT

The use of the term "quality dimension" is synonymous to the term "customer requirements." Customer requirements specifically represent the attributes or features of a product or service that the customer deems important in achieving his or her customer satisfaction. Clearly, a customer can perceive several attributes and these attributes may differ from product to product and from service to service. However, certain industries have universal attributes. For example, in the auto industry, attributes such as safety are always important to the customer. In the service sector for example, Kennedy and Young (1989) identified four common attributes or quality dimension as availability, responsiveness, convenience, and timeliness. Authors of SERVQUAL model present five dimensions of service quality as tangibles, reliability, responsiveness, assurance, and empathy (Parasuraman, Zeithaml, & Berry, 1988). These quality dimensions are, however, specific to service organizations. Through extensive literature reviews, members of the cross-functional teams for QFD can identify specific quality dimensions for their particular industries. However, such dimensions of quality may not cover all the important attributes or customer requirements for a specific product. It is, therefore, important to go beyond the "generic industry attributes" to identify specifically the attributes of the product that the customer needs. Thus, there is a need for the cross-functional team to conduct a detailed study of the product or service to identify other hidden attributes. Such studies employ knowledgeable experts and focus customer groups who understand the product and are able to offer insights on the customer's expectations of the product. Through this, a list of quality attributes can be identified. It is important also, to conduct benchmarking analysis to identify other attributes present in competitor's products. The attributes identified must be clearly stated to avoid ambiguities. For example, important consumer research publications that do comparative analysis of products could be important sources of information since such publications often compare similar products by looking at quality attributes that are important to customers.

The quality dimension approach relies heavily on the cross-functional teams as experts who know and understand the product's purpose or function. Such teams could therefore, breakdown the product into its functional components and study and analyze it to see how the needs of the customer are satisfied. Suppose we take an auto manufacturer as an example, a sample of customer requirement issues may include the following:

Operational:	The ease of opening the car door.
Operational:	The length of time or mileage between scheduled service.
Aesthetics:	The size or shape of the car.
Availability of Support:	The ease to which service can be obtained.
Responsiveness:	The time it takes to perform scheduled service.

These attributes can be grouped into keywords or dimensions of quality and each evaluated to eliminate redundancies. The cross-functional team can now work with specific quality dimensions that cover a range of customer requirement issues. In addition to these attributes which we have referred to in Chapter 1 as the "spoken requirements," there are "unspoken requirements" that the members of the cross-functional teams must also identify and ensure that they are present in the product. For example, certain levels of safety should be guaranteed; the car should meet emission laws; the car must have an aesthetic appeal; the price should be reasonable; etc. Thus, both "spoken" and "unspoken" requirements should be present.

When a long list of attributes is generated, it is possible that some of the attributes may not be important or may add little or no value to the product. Rather than the team wasting valuable resources to tackle insignificant problems, it is important that some method be devised to assign priorities to the customer requirements that have been identified. The focus should be on solving the critical and important problems. It is more important to include the major customer requirements in a satisfying manner to the customer than to marginally consider every conceivable factor. We shall now discuss the critical incident approach.

CRITICAL INCIDENT APPROACH

Flanagan (1954) developed this approach. It could be used to develop customer satisfaction questionnaires to understand customer requirements.

This method views organizational performance from the perspective of the customer. The customer views organizational performance from the aspects of the organization it is directly in contact with. With respect to manufacturing, the customer is in direct contact with the product. And, with respect to service, the customer is in direct contact with the staff. The customer looks at the product or service attribute on how the attribute may positively or negatively affect organizational performance. An attribute that will have a negative effect would impact on the customer's positive perception of the organization thereby, negatively affecting organizational performance. However, an attribute that has a positive impact will be more desirable to the customer. Critical incidents are therefore, the "quality attributes" of the organization that the customer is directly in contact with. These critical incidents could be obtained either through individual or group interviewing. This process is conducted by dealing directly with people who have used the product or service and are in a position to offer specific judgments on the different attributes of the product or service. It is recommended that between 10 to 20 customers be interviewed and each customer should be asked to describe 5 to 10 positive and negative instances for the product or service respectively (Hayes, 1992). In addition, the questions should be specific and avoid the use of general terms. This should help the customer to focus on specifics. The use of a large number of customers helps to reduce the possibility of obtaining incomplete information. For example, information not obtained from one interviewee can be compensated from subsequent interviews with other customers. From the interviewing process, a list of critical incidents could be developed which can be grouped again into specific "quality attributes."

ANALYSIS OF QUALITY ATTRIBUTES

It is important to solve the critical problem. A major problem that may arise from using these techniques to solicit customer requirements is that a long list may be generated that may be unmanageable. Our recommendation will be to identify both the "spoken" and "unspoken" product or service attributes through these methods. Organize the attributes into quality dimensions and develop a "customer satisfaction survey" to relate these quality attributes to the specific product or service. The aim should be to identify from a more typical group which customer requirements are important. The survey should be administered to a random sample of existing and potential customers. The survey should be analyzed statistically to identify which quality attributes are significant or important in achieving customer satisfaction. This will help to narrow down the list of "critical incidents" to quality attributes that a typical group of the customer base views as important. The cross-functional team can then focus its effort in satisfying those significant requirements. This approach will help the cross-functional team address the most important customer requirement issues, save time, and optimize the use of limited resources.

National City Bank Uses QFD to Work Out IT

QFD has been applied by National City Corporation to help in identifying and prioritize the needs of its customers and in evaluating each project based on its contributed benefit to meet these needs. The projects are subsequently assessed for degree of complexity, and for helping IT department managers to assign resources appropriately. National City developed a list of internal customer needs, creating the criteria for determining project benefit, and then developed a separate set of criteria to judge project complexity and the required technical skills to work on the project. Upon completing this process, National City can now prioritize its internal IT projects and staff them with the most appropriate people, thus delivering the greatest value to National City's customers (LePrevost & Glenn, 2003).

CONCLUSION

In this chapter, we have discussed issues relating to the "voice of the customer." We discussed the formation of cross-functional teams to identify customer requirements from a product or service. In addition, we noted potential benefits and problems with the use of cross-functional teams and the need to focus on overall organizational goals. We note the two important methods to identify customer requirements namely: quality dimension development and critical incident approach. We conclude by emphasizing the use of questionnaire surveys administered to a random sample of customers to identify significant customer requirement issues. This will help the cross-functional QFD team to focus on the most important customer requirement issues, better utilize its resources, and timely design and produce the product and service needed by its customers.

SELF STUDY QUESTIONS

1. What are the three levels in listening to the "Voice of the Customer?" Give a short explanation with relevant example.
2. What is the purpose of cross functional team? What are the problems associated with them?
3. What are the methods to identify customer requirements?

REFERENCES

Flanagan, M. (1954). The critical incident technique. *Psychological Bulletin, 51,* 327–358.

Hayes, B. E. (1992). *Measuring customer satisfaction: Development and use of questionnaires.* Milwaukee, WI: ASQC Quality Press.

Kennedy, D. A., & Young, B. J. (1989). Managing quality in staff areas. *Quality Progress, 22*(10), 87–91.

LePrevost, J., & Glenn, M. (2003). Quality infrastructure improvement: Using QFD to manage project priorities and project management resources. Retrieved from http://mazur.net/works/national_city_bank_it_project_selection_qfd.pdf

Parasuraman, A., Zeithaml, V. A., & Berry, L. L. (1988). SERVQUAL: A multiple-item scale for measuring customer perceptions of service quality. *Journal of Retailing, 64,* 12–40.

Vonderembse, M. A., & Van Fossen, T. (1998). Quality function deployment. In C. N. Madu (Ed.), *Handbook of total quality management.* Boston, MA: Kluwer.

CHAPTER 3

IDENTIFYING CUSTOMER NEEDS

In the previous chapter, we briefly discussed how customer requirements can be identified. Knowing what the customer wants is a critical part of quality function deployment. Although we have discussed the use of critical incident approach where the customer can identify the positive and negative attributes of the product or services, we want to discuss in this chapter, the use of other methods to identify customer requirements. Properly identifying the customer requirement is mission-critical and will inform the ability to continue to satisfy and maintain loyal customers.

As mentioned in the previous chapter, customer needs are "spoken" and "unspoken." However, they play significant role in determining customer satisfaction when they interact with the products and services offered by the business. It is therefore important to obtain feedback from the customer as the customer goes through the several processes of product or service delivery. By being able to provide top class products or services, the business will enrich the experience of customers, increase customer satisfaction, and maintain loyal customers. We can therefore identify why it is important to know the needs of the customer.

Knowing Customer Needs

- Businesses survive by building customer loyalty. This can be achieved only when customer satisfaction is ensured. The business

The House of Quality in a Minute:
A Guide to Quality Function Deployment (3rd Ed.), pp. 19–31
Copyright © 2020 by Information Age Publishing
All rights of reproduction in any form reserved.

environment is very competitive. If customers are not satisfied, they will try other competitors. It is important and cheaper to retain existing customers than to attract new customers.

- Customer needs are unique. It is not one size fits all especially in the delivery of services. We need to be responsive and adapt to satisfy the needs of the customer. It will be erroneous to assume that all customers have the same basic needs.

- Cross-selling of products or services can be carried out when the needs of customers are known.

- In listening to the voice of the customer, it is also important to be able to respond effectively to their questions and concerns. Sometimes, customers may not be clear on their needs. It is imperative that efforts are made to assist them on how the products or services that are offered can help them to enrich their experiences.

- A satisfied customer is a valuable asset to the business. They talk good about the product or service, provide useful feedback that may guide prospective customers, they are less likely to engage in dispute or legal actions against the business, and they can be counted on as repeat customers. Their loyalty is key to sustaining the business and helping it to thrive and develop new products and services to continue to enrich the experiences of their customers.

- Listening to the voice of the customer helps the business to understand the shortcomings of its products and services and develop means of improving the product or services to continue to meet the needs of the customer.

How to Identify Customer Needs

There are several ways customer needs can be identified. Information derived can help not only in designing and marketing new products or services but also in improving existing products and services. Businesses must continue to listen to the voice of the customer and use the information discerned from that to continue to improve its services. We briefly discuss some of the methods that are frequently used ("Identifying and Meeting," n.d.; Linton, 2019):

- **Market Research—**
  Market research is one of the older techniques that have been used to get information on customer needs and preferences. This may take different forms. It may include the use of questionnaire surveys, collection of feedbacks from customer, telephone and online surveys, review of published reports available in consumer

reports, and even visits to customer's websites. Market research can help to detect things like demographic changes, trends, and even changes in purchasing behavior. Opportunities may be identified through this that may enable the business to continue to meet the needs of the customer.

- **Review of Historical Data—**

  Businesses maintain customer historical data. These could be in the form of past surveys, customer feedbacks, or customer interviews. The past will usually inform on the future. However, it may still be necessary to update the data since patterns may have changed. In this era or Big Data, there are data analytics tools that can be employed to huge databases to be able to isolate customer needs. The historical data is therefore essential in identifying customer needs.

- **Social Media—**

  There is an avalanche of information that flow through the social media. Businesses can use the information available on social media to get understanding of both customer perceptions of their products and customer needs. There is information on customer feedback and ongoing discussions that may relate to the products and services that are offered. It is important to engage in such discussions and try to understand the views of the customer and also provide clarifications when necessary.

- **Engaging Stakeholders—**

  Stakeholders should include who we refer to as active participants. They are those who are affected by or may affect the product or services. The stakeholder definition here in inclusive and it is not restricted only to the internal employees of the business. We should engage the salespeople who are at the field and have more frequent contact with customers to work with customers and other interest groups to identify the needs of the customer. We should point out that the needs of the customer may go beyond the direct services a product may provide to the customer but may also include issues such as the materials that are used in making the product and how environmentally friendly, they may be. This approach encourages collaboration with customers and other stakeholders in designing a product that will reflect their needs. It will ensure the stakeholders buy-in and reduces the possibility of resistance or rejection of the product. Of course, not every single customer will be involved but a representative group of customers can join in forming a project team to address customer requirements.

o **Customer Feedback**—Businesses like to hear from their verified customers on how they are doing. Feedback provides insight on how well the product or service is satisfying customer needs. It helps businesses to critically assess the product and understand the features or attributes that the customer finds useful and areas of discomfort. Customers may also be encouraged to join online user groups where they can offer suggestions on how the product or service can be improved.

o **Keyword Research**—With a stroke of the key, one can go online and search for virtually anything from the search engines like google. This also provides information on the needs of the customer. The question is, what do people frequently search online about the product or service? What are the responses they also get online about their search? There may be comments left by other customers that can explain the issues reflected in the keyword search. Businesses need to know that and make good use of this vital source of information on customer needs.

Sauro (2015) noted ten methods for identifying customer needs. Some of these have been discussed above. However, we are going to briefly discuss some of the other ones not yet listed above.

- **Mapping the customer process**—This involves using a process map to enrich customer experience. An example provided may account to one of the reasons Uber has been successful. Prior to Uber, there was actually a disconnect between the customer and the taxi or cab company. Contact was usually over the phone where a customer calls up the company and was told how long it will take for a cab to arrive. The cab fare is also often not known until the meter is turned on and the customer reaches the destination. However, Uber provides real time services where both the cab driver and the customer will know the location of each other, have a map directing the driver to the passenger and actually showing the passenger the location of the cab. Furthermore, payments are charged and paid on a credit card without the customer worrying of being overcharged because the driver may have taken the longer route. This Uber case exemplifies what the process is for catching a cab. However, there is process in every activity and it is important to always map out the process to see how it can be streamlined and improved. One popular way for mapping out a process is to use flow charts to draw out the processes involved and then query the process by asking what value each process creates to the customer. Non-value adding processes can be removed to enrich

the customer experience. Figures 3.1a and 3.1b are simple flow
charts depicting the traditional cab and Uber processes. It is clear
from this flow chart that Uber has a streamlined process. Further,
there is room for customer dissatisfaction with the traditional cab
demand process. The dissatisfaction may result from not knowing
exactly how long to wait for a cab or where the cab is? There is also
possible dissatisfaction over payment of fare since the true value
may not be known prior to the ride. Mapping out the customer
process may therefore help to not only understand how the process
works but also to understand how it can be streamlined and
improved on.

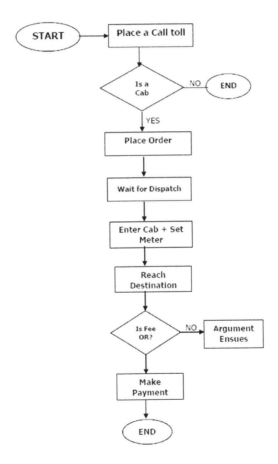

Figure 3.1a.   Traditional Cab Service.

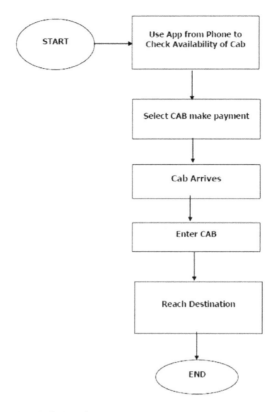

Figure 3.1b.   UBER Cab Service.

- **Mapping the customer journey**—The process of a customer patronizing a product or service is seen as a journey. It is a journey that will turn the customer from a prospective buyer to a verified buyer. It is good practice to also map out this process using a flow diagram to understand the decision-making process that may be involved, to provide solutions and explanations to potential concerns of the customer, and to use the information gained at this stage to continue to improve customer experience. Customers do not want to make the wrong choices. They take time to review and assess competitive products on different criteria. Issues of warranty, return policies, serviceability, dependability, and reliability may be points of concern and they may need clarity on them. They may also express their desires and such information can be used to achieve improvement in product and service delivery.

- **Follow me home**—This requires following a customer home or to work to observe how the customer uses the product and to identify areas for improvement. Sauro (2015) note how Intuit was able to improve the point-of-sale (POS) cash registrar for retail customers. By following these customers to their work, a team from Intuit observed the difficulty the retailers were having in exporting transactions from their POS to QuickBooks. Subsequently, they were able to integrate QuickBooks into cash registrars thus eliminating the need to export transaction data.

- **Analyze your competition**—It is important to know your competitors and know what they are up to. Competitors may not always come from the same industry, but they may be providing competing products and services. A popularly used technique for analyzing competition is the SWOT analysis. SWOT means Strengths, Weaknesses, Opportunities, and Threats. Strengths and Weaknesses are considered to be internal to the organization while Opportunities and Threats are external to the organization. Figure 3.2 shows a SWOT diagram. By analyzing your competition, you can go further to position yourself in a grid that shows where you are relative to your competitors. This positioning actually is indicative of how customer needs are not being satisfied. This is shown in Figure 3.3. We adapt the work of Tenner and Detoro (1997) and shown in the Figure 3.3 matrix how a firm can position itself against its competitors. There are four positions in this grid namely Unhealthy, Satisfactory, Superior, and World-class. The world-class companies are those to benchmark and copy from. No one wants to find itself in an unhealthy position. The firm wants to move up to the world-class position and must learn what it takes to be in that position. Those currently in that position, must continue to innovate and enrich customer experiences so they are not overtaken by competitors. The key point here is that you want to be a world-class competitor. This cannot be achieved if you lag behind in satisfying customer needs. Benchmarking is exceedingly necessary at this stage to understand where you are and to assess what it will take you to get to where you want to be. If in the short run, it is not possible to get to where you want to be, you may consider subcontracting part of that activity to those that have core competence in it.

Figure 3.2. SWOT Analysis.

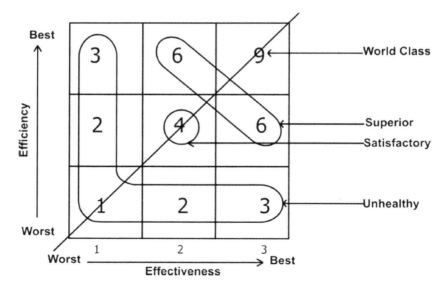

Figure 3.3. Efficiency vs Effectiveness Matrix.

An example of SWOT is presented below:

- *Internal*
  - o Strengths
    Core competence within the organization
    Quality processes
    Financial stability
  - o Weaknesses
    Lack of skilled professionals
    Poor quality
    Out-dated and inefficient processes
    Poor work environment

- *External*
  - o Opportunities
    New market to tap from such as e-learning
    Possibility of strategic alliances
    Changing competitive landscape
    Globalization
  - o *Threats*
    New entrants such as online academic programs, short courses
    Price fluctuations i.e., tuition plans by other institutions
    Increased number of competitors

- **Cause-and-effect relationships**—It is important to understand the cause-and-effect relationship. For example, what will cause a customer to be dissatisfied with the product or service? In any analysis of this form, there are four main causes and they are Man, Machine, Material, and Method or rather 4Ms. This approach is widely used in the literature and is often referred to as the Ishikawa diagram or the Fish bone diagram. We shall illustrate this using an example of a student dissatisfaction with the university services. But first, Man refers to all the errors that may be attributed to Human involvement in the product or service delivery process; Machine refers to the technological process itself that is used to provide the products and services; Material refers to problems with the actual materials that are used; and Method deals with the process and policies to provide goods and services. Figure 3.4 provides an example of student dissatisfaction. We can analyze that by using the fish bone diagram where we break the problem into four Ms. Machinery for example identifies uncomfortable classrooms, banner system, inadequate computers or smart rooms. The problems identified under each M are listed in the diagram. These represent the customer needs that must be satisfied in order to achieve student satisfaction. This approach can therefore help in problem solving to identify the needs of the customer.

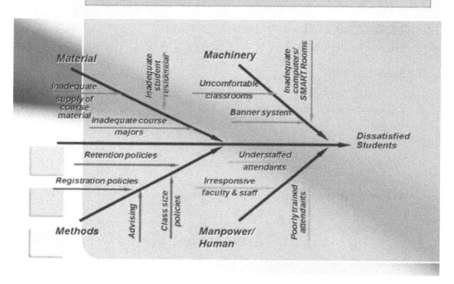

Figure 3.4.   Fish Bone Diagram.

Meeting Customer Needs

The needs that have been identified must be satisfied. The primary way to satisfy these needs is to integrate them in design hence the use of quality function deployment. However, the design process will also require customer engagement at the different phases of design. Meeting these needs can be better described using the Plan-Do-Check-Act.

Plan—the customer needs that are generated through the different approaches discussed above are made available to product or service designers within the firm. There may also be a team that handles the designing of products or services. The information is carefully studied to find an efficient way to satisfy those needs.

Do—the products or services benefitting from this information are then developed on a small scale and a pilot study is conducted to identify areas for improvement.

Check—Data collected from the pilot study are analyzed and areas for improvement are identified and amendments are made.

Act—It is now time to introduce a full-blown products or services for the market. It is imperative to continue to collect information, feedback, and continue to listen to the voice of the customer on how to continue to satisfy their needs. The PDCA is a cyclic process to continue to achieve improvements over time. This is shown in Figure 3.5.

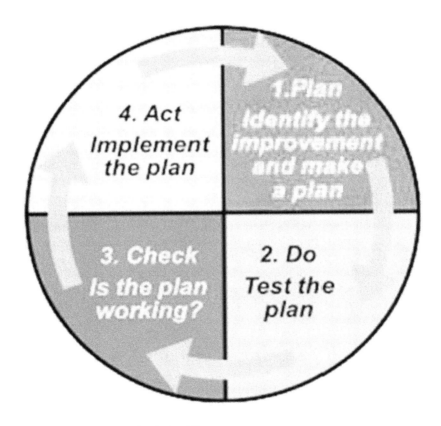

Figure 3.5.   Plan-Do-Check-Act Diagram.

Uber vs. Taxis: Meeting and Exceeding Consumer Needs
Uber has separated itself from traditional taxis by meeting and exceeding customer needs. It does this by offering services that the customer wants. These services were not attainable from the traditional taxis. Thus, Uber revolutionized the taxi services by offering the following: frictionless payments and receipts—Uber accepts credit card payments for the ride and tips and the receipts are generally e-mailed to the customer. It makes requesting for taxi very convenient and the cabs can be tracked on a real time basis with information on the location and arrival of the cab shown virtually on the Uber app in the customer's cell phone. Uber cars especially the UberX which are personal vehicles are noted to be very clean and actually cleaner on the average than the traditional taxis. These cars are often times new. Customer experience has been reported to be better than the traditional cabs. There is more credibility, trust, and transparency. The customer knows the information about the driver and the car to be transported on. There is also trust that you will not be exploited especially in an unfamiliar area. The customer also has the opportunity to rate his or her overall customer experience. Thus, the voice of the customer is heard and listened to in order to improve services. Uber's prices are competitive and are generally cheaper than the traditional cab fares. Uber embraces the Procter & Gamble mantra "Consumer is Boss." This has helped it to continue to add value to its services and enrich customer experience (Ryan, 2013).

CONCLUSION

Identifying customer needs is mission-critical. It is the essence of being able to satisfy the customer and maintaining customer loyalty. This chapter discussed the importance of knowing customer needs, showed different approaches to identify customer needs, and recommends different ways to integrate these needs in a design strategy that will encourage stakeholder participation. It goes without saying that successful businesses are those who can satisfy the needs of their customers. We present a case of Uber a cab service company that has transformed the way taxis operate worldwide. In this case, we identify the needs of the customer that Uber has been able to satisfy and that has made Uber to become a world class business in its sector. Businesses need to be innovative and identify the niche that is currently not being satisfied. If they can satisfy such niche, they will enrich customer experience and be able to maintain loyal customers.

SELF STUDY QUESTIONS

1. Map out a process to identify customer needs and potential bottlenecks for a product or service of interest to you. How can you streamline the process?
2. There are different methods for identifying customer needs. Select one of them and discuss how you can apply it in your product or service needs.
3. SWOT analysis can be used to analyze customer needs. Discuss how you can apply it in your workplace to satisfy customer needs.

REFERENCES

Ryan, P. (2013). Uber vs. Taxis: Meeting and exceeding consumer needs. October 23, 2018, from http://www.denneen.com/2015/09/04/uber-vs-taxis-meeting-and-exceeding-consumer-needs/ Presentation is adapted from this paper.

Identifying and meeting customer needs. (n.d.). In *Conductor.* Retrieved from https://www.conductor.com/learning-center/customer-needs/

Linton, I. (2019). Strategies for identifying customer needs. Retrieved from https://smallbusiness.chron.com/strategies-identifying-customer-needs-54317.html

Sauro, J. (2015). *Customer analytics for dummies.* Hoboken, NJ: John Wiley & Sons.

Tenner, A. R., & DeToro, I. J. (1996). *Process redesign: The implementation guide for managers.* Boston, MA: Addison Wesley.

CHAPTER 4

HOUSE OF QUALITY

In this chapter, we discuss how to build the "House of Quality." In Chapter 2, we discussed how product or service characteristics that are important to the customer can be identified. However, these product characteristics must be integrated into the design of the product. Charts are important in building the House of Quality. By using charts or diagrams, information obtained by listening to the "voice of the customer" can be summarized and compared to design requirements. The House of Quality is therefore, a blueprint for product development. We shall breakdown in a stepwise form, how the House of Quality can be built.

Step 1: In Chapter 2, we identified customer requirements. We also noted that this could be an extensive list and it is important to identify the significant requirements and eliminate any redundancies that may exist. A list of the important customer requirements should be constructed and should include product or service attributes as identified by customers. This list is often referred to as "whats" to signify what the customer actually wants to see in a product or service. However, care must be taken to ensure that these "whats" can be made operational. For example, consider the subscription to Internet Online servers. It is not enough for a customer to state that he or she needs a "reliable or good online service." The term "reliable or good" is broad and should be broken down to attributes that could be used to define such an adjective. For example, a good online server may have the following attributes: local access numbers, support

The House of Quality in a Minute:
A Guide to Quality Function Deployment (3rd Ed.), pp. 33–41
Copyright © 2020 by Information Age Publishing

33

for a wide range of modems, accessible online and telephone help, easy access to Internet, ease of access to the server, etc. Thus, the "whats" of a customer must be broken down to primary, secondary, and tertiary levels of information. It is apparent that the primary objective in this example is to have a good or reliable online server. However, the attributes used to qualify the adjective "good" are secondary and must be present to achieve the primary objective. These secondary objectives can be further broken down to tertiary levels of information. For example, "ease of access to the server" may include offering several local access numbers that the user can dial up if one is busy or the use of cable modems or DSL. The list of "whats" as identified by the customer should be clearly defined.

Step 2: Once this list of "whats" is clarified, a list of the design requirements known as the "hows" should be developed. This list of "hows" shows how design requirements can influence the attainment of "whats" as identified by the customer. The design characteristics are often under the control of the manufacturer or the producer and are at times, referred to as "engineering characteristics." They could be expressed in technical terms within the organization and are measurable. For example, what is the maximum transfer rate of information that the server provides (i.e., 11mbps). This could partly measure the ease of access to the Internet or World Wide Web. This step involves the translation of customer requirements to design requirements. This process is compounded by the fact that there may exist interdependent relationships between design requirements. In other words, some of the design requirements may conflict with each other or rather, the "hows" may negatively influence one another. However, this is to be expected because there are multiple goals identified in the "whats" and in trying to achieve all these goals, there will be some tradeoffs. If such conflicts do not exist, it is possible that an error has been committed. A well-designed product or service is likely to involve tradeoffs (American Supplier Institute, 1989). Potential conflicts that are identified must be resolved productively. With the use of QFD, such conflicts can be effectively resolved during the product design stage thereby, reducing the need for significant engineering changes downstream.

Step 3: Steps 1 and 2 form the basis for the first QFD chart (Figure 3.1). Figure 4.1 has several components. First, this figure contains the list of significant customer requirements (whats) shown on the left side of the matrix as rows and a list of design requirements (hows) listed in columns. The definitions of the symbols used to show the relationship between a customer requirement and a design requirement are presented. For example, a Δ symbol shown at an intersection point between customer requirement and design requirement means the weakest design requirement to satisfy that customer requirement. Figure 4.1 also contains a column titled "importance to customer." This column denotes the relative importance of the customer

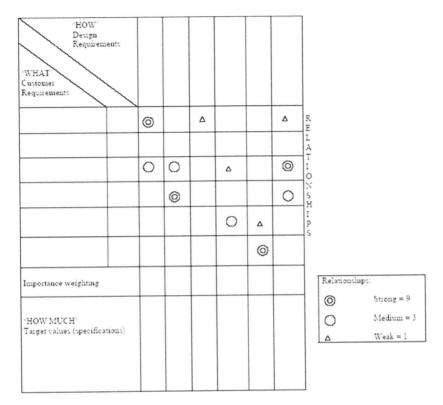

Figure 4.1.   QFD Relationship Matrix.

requirement attributes to the customer. This will help designers focus more attention on achieving those attributes that are of utmost importance to the customer. The Figure 4.1 also has at the bottom, the target values or specifications or "how much," and a row that contains the importance weighting. The importance weighting at the bottom is similar to the "importance to customer" column. This denotes the importance for the different design requirements. The target values are the specifications that could be achieved through engineering design. For example, suppose that one customer requirement in a new car is the "ease to close the car door." A design requirement may be to investigate the "energy requirement to close the door," and the target specification may be to reduce energy level to 7.5ft/lb (Hauser & Clausing, 1988). Thus, the target values deal with the 'how much' or specifics. The QFD cross-functional team generates these values, as they believe them to satisfy customer requirements. Design requirements must be compared to measurable targets that are under the control of the designer.

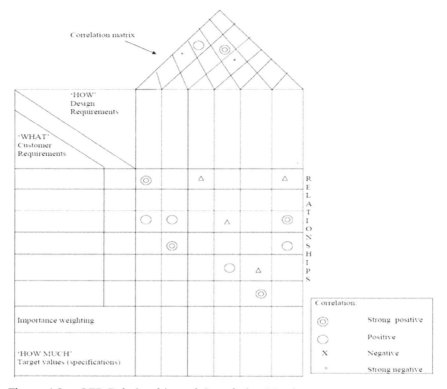

Figure 4.2.   QFD Relationship and Correlation Matrix.

Step 4: Figure 4.2 is used to illustrate this step. This involves the addition of the correlation matrix to actually form a "house" or rather, the house of quality. This correlation matrix shows the correlation between the different design requirements. On the right side of Figure 4.2 is the definition of the symbols used for the correlation. For example, the use of the symbol * denotes strong negative correlation between two design requirements and x denotes negative correlation. Of utmost importance is the negative and strong negative correlation observed between the design requirements. Such relationships imply that there is a conflict in trying to achieve both requirements jointly. Thus, as one is being achieved, the other is being compromised. This conflict needs to be resolved or a trade-off decision must be made. Such decision could involve retaining the design requirement that has the higher importance weighting.

Step 5: Figure 4.3 is a modification of Figure 4.2 to include two new components namely "competitive evaluation" and "technical evaluation." These two offer a benchmarking of the manufacturer's product or service to that of competitors in several ways. For example, with the competitive

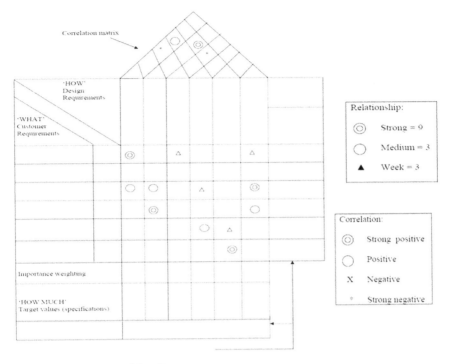

Figure 4.3.   House of Quality.

evaluation, the manufacturer is compared to its competitors on each of the customer requirements identified by the customer. Similarly, for the technical evaluation, the manufacturer is compared against its competitors based on the design requirements to satisfy customer requirements. One thing not shown yet in this diagram is that the manufacturer is positioned in a scale against its competitors. Ideally, the manufacturer will like to out-perform its competitors. Thus, the manufacturer must make the effort to be the best in class. To put all these in perspective, we shall illustrate with an example. Figure 4.4 is adapted from the case presented by Hauser and Clausing (1988).

A CASE EXAMPLE

We shall adapt the example presented by Hauser and Clausing (1988). In that example, they showed that for a particular product, series of subcharts could be created. For example, they considered developing the QFD for the door of an automobile. This alone will require its own QFD chart, which eventually could be tied in with the other QFDs that may be needed to build a quality automobile. Customer attributes for a car door are developed and grouped as primary, secondary and tertiary. Thus, the example presented below and demonstrated in other sections of this book will focus on designing and building a quality car door to satisfy customer requirements.

Using Figure 4.4, we can determine the importance weighting for the design requirements. For example, consider the design requirement "energy needed to close door." This design requirement is strongly related to the customer requirement "easy to close" and modestly related to "easy to open." We can determine its importance weighting as $(7 \times 9) + (3 \times 3) = 72$ where the strong relationship is rated as 9 and the moderate relationship is rated as 3. The "importance to customer" weights are 7 and 3 respectively. Similarly, we can determine the other importance weights as 72, 57, 43, 9, 6, and 45 respectively.

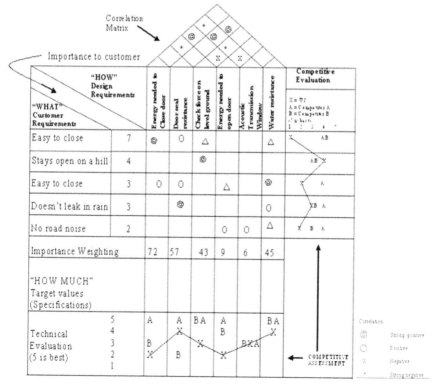

Figure 4.4.   QFD Example.

Thus, in terms of importance, we can order the design requirements as follows: energy needed to close door, door seal resistance, water resistance, check force on level ground, energy needed to open door, and acoustic transmission window. We also notice that there are some negative correlations. For example, energy needed to close door is strongly negatively correlated to check force on level ground. Thus, this conflict must be resolved, or a trade-off must be made. In terms of trade-off, it is seen from the importance weighting that the energy needed to close door is more important than check force on level ground. Similarly, this example shows that door seal resistance is positively correlated with water resistance.

The other important information that is gained here is the competitive assessment information. As seen from the information provided, this manufacturer is the worst in the first "customer requirement" which is "easy to close door" and worst on "easy to open" and "no road noise." However, it appears to be the best on the "customer requirement" "stays open on a hill." The Xs are all connected to help position the manufacturer against its competitors. We can also derive similar interpretations for the technical evaluation.

The steps outlined so far are useful for documentation purposes. They present the requirements the product should have to satisfy customer requirements but the House of Quality as shown here, does not represent product design. This process could be taken further to link it to other QFD activities within the organization. For example, engineering or design requirements could be further broken down to parts characteristics which may be broken down to key process operations down to production requirements (Vonderembse & Van Fossen, 1998). It is important to note that the deployment of information is not unidirectional but iterative. For example, modifications on the QFD obtain at the early stage may be necessitated from the information acquired at a later stage. The stepwise approach to link the different QFD charts helps to trace information backward to the original customer demands.

Multilevel House of Quality

With the use of QFD, quality efforts can be deployed by creating several inter-related "House" where output from one house serves as Input into another house. The overriding goal of QFD is to satisfy customer requirements through design specifications. However, this broader objective can be broken-down into operational forms that show systematic process of satisfying customer requirements. The result of this inter-related HOUSES OF QUALITY that feed onto each other. A typical example of house resources are deployed to achieve customer requirements is presented in Figure 4.5.

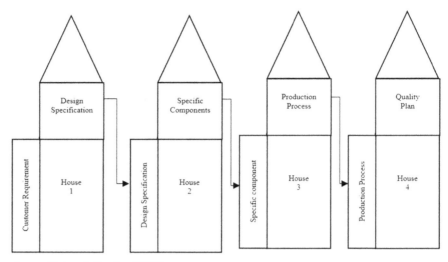

Source: Heizer & Render (2010).

Figure 4.5.   House resources.

CONCLUSION

In this chapter, we discussed how to build the House of Quality. We showed that this is done graphically by developing charts to organize "customer requirements" and "engineering or design requirements" needed to satisfy the customer. We also showed by example how to interpret information from the QFD chart. We must caution however, that the example is for illustrative purposes only. Furthermore, different organizations may modify the QFD chart to better suit their needs. We also noted that QFD is an iterative process that requires linking each phase. The procedures are similar however, every stage may involve its own QFD chart. For example, there may be a need for a QFD chart for design requirements as they will be met by "parts characteristics" and "parts characteristics" as they will be satisfied by "key process operations" and so on. By linking all these different QFD charts, it becomes easier to trace information back to their original sources. Although the final QFD charts may look complicated, they are not difficult to generate once the relevant information is available.

SELF STUDY QUESTIONS

1. What are the steps to build the House of Quality? Please explain briefly.
2. What is the prerequisite to House of Quality?

3. How would you go about building house of quality to better meet the needs of your customers? Discuss what their needs are and how you would be able to satisfy them. What would be your most important design strategy to satisfy the most important customer needs?

REFERENCES

American Supplier Institute. (1989). *Quality function deployment implementation manual*. Dearborn, MI: American Supplier Institute.

Hauser, J. R., & Clausing, D. (1988, May–June). The house of quality. *Harvard Business Review*, pp. 62–73.

Heizer, J., & Render, B. (2010). *Operations management* (10th ed.). Upper Saddle River, NJ: Prentice Hall.

Vonderembse, M. A., & Van Fossen, T. (1998). Quality function deployment. In C. N. Madu (Ed.), *Handbook of total quality management*. Boston, MA: Kluwer.

CHAPTER 5

QFD AND THE ANALYTIC
HIERARCHY PROCESS (AHP)

Chapter 4 illustrates how to build the House of Quality. Apart from identifying customer requirements for a product or service and developing the list of design requirements to satisfy such needs, we noticed the QFD charts contain relative weights on the customer requirements. Also, the chart contains benchmarking information. In this chapter, we shall focus on the relative weights that are assigned to customer requirements.

The main purpose of assigning relative weights to the customer requirements is to make sure the customer's priorities are integrated in the product design. Obviously, these critical requirements are the ones that customers will frequently look for in the product or service. Once these important requirements are absent, the customer can not be satisfied. Clearly, there are several requirements that the customer may want present in a product. However, the manufacturer is operating with limited resources and may not be able to satisfy all these needs. It is therefore, important to focus on the most important needs of the customer. Furthermore, even when it may be possible to satisfy all the customer requirements, it is important to the manufacturer to identify the most critical needs of the customer. Due attention should be paid to ensure that such requirements are integrated in the product design.

The House of Quality in a Minute:
A Guide to Quality Function Deployment (3rd Ed.), pp. 43–55
Copyright © 2020 by Information Age Publishing

In the example we presented in Chapter 4 (Figure 4.4), we assigned weights to customer requirement items to show the importance of these items to the customer. For example, a weight of 7 was assigned to "easy to close" while a weight of 2 was assigned to "no road noise." These weights show for example that "easy to close" is more important to the customer than "no road noise." There are, however, potential problems with this method of assignment. First, such assignment could become arbitrary if there is no structured approach to reach to these numbers. Second, with several customer requirements to consider at the same time, it may be difficult to arrive at a meaningful weight assignment. Third, it may be difficult to measure the consistency of the decision maker(s) that assigns these weights. Yet, as we saw from Figure 4.4, these weight assignments are critical in deriving useful information from the QFD chart. For example, the importance weighting obtained for the design requirements are influenced by the 'importance to customer' weights that were used. Thus, if these weights are inaccurately assigned, the organization will focus on the insignificant design requirements and will therefore, design products that may not meet customer requirements.

What we intend to do is present a structured approach to assign the "importance to customer" weights. These weights will then be validated in terms of their consistency. The process used for this purpose is known as the "Analytic Hierarchy Process" or AHP for short.

Briefly, the AHP is "a multi-criteria decision model that uses hierarchic or network structure to represent a decision problem and then develops priorities for alternatives based on the decision maker's judgment throughout the system" (Saaty, 1987, p. 157). Figure 5.1 that depicts a network of customer requirements is an example. Here, the goal is to determine the relative importance of these customer requirement items to the customer.

The AHP has been used in many decision-making contexts and it is quite applicable for QFD application for the following reasons:

1. The AHP is based on pairwise comparison between competing alternatives. For example, each QFD team member can take only a pair of customer requirements and compare at a time (i.e., "easy to close" compared to 'stays open on a hill' in terms of their relative importance to the customer). This pairwise comparison reduces the number of customer requirement items that each member must consider at any one time to be able to assign a relative importance weight.
2. It allows for the consideration of both objective (i.e., the price of a product) and subjective (i.e., customer's perception of a product characteristic) factors.

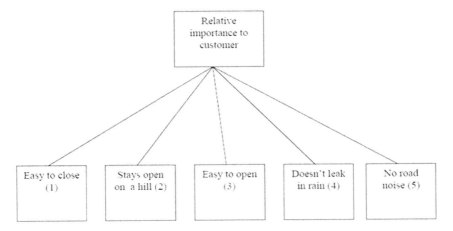

Figure 5.1. Customer requirement importance rating.

3. The consistency in the judgment of the QFD team members could be easily derived and the quality of their judgment can be evaluated. Although consistency does not infer quality decisions, however, all quality decisions are consistent. When the QFD team members' judgments are consistent, there will be a greater likelihood that quality decisions will be reached. In other words, it will be more likely that the weight assigned to customer requirements may reflect the importance of these requirements to the customer.

4. As we alluded in Chapters 1 and 2, QFD team is comprised of cross-functional departments. Clearly, with multiple people involved in the decision-making process, it becomes much harder to obtain a single number that will denote their agreed importance weight to a customer requirement item. It is better that each member assigns his or her own weight independently to avoid the weights being "biased" from "group-think" syndrome. The AHP allows each member to independently assign weights to the customer requirements and then, these weights are combined to arrive at a group index.

5. Conflict resolution is an important part of QFD. We noted in the case of design requirements where there may be a need for trade-off. However, conflict may be as a result of the significance of some of the customer requirement items. Such conflicts can easily be identified through AHP (Madu, 1994) and other management techniques could be used jointly with AHP to resolve such conflicts.

We shall now, apply the AHP to the same problem we covered in Chapter 4 and shown as Figure 4.4. Table 5.1 illustrates a pairwise comparison matrix for the customer requirements. The customer requirements are codified as 1 = easy to close; 2 = stays open on a hill; 3 = easy to open; 4 = does not leak in rain; and 5 = no road noise. Thus, when an item is compared to itself, its relative importance over itself is 1. When however, easy to close (1) is compared to easy to open (3), the relative importance of (1) over (3) is 7 which means that "easy to close" has very strong importance over "easy to open." Each QFD team member conducts his or her own pairwise comparison of the customer requirement items. The QFD team assignment is obtained by taking a geometric mean of all team members assignment for each pair of comparison. The weighting scale used in AHP are defined as follows: 1 = equal importance; 3 = moderate importance of one customer requirement item over the other; 5 = strong importance; 7 = very strong importance; and 9 = extreme importance. The even numbers 2, 4, 6, and 8 are used for compromise, while reciprocals are used to show inverse comparisons.

Table 5.1.
Pair Wise Comparison of Customer Requirements

	1	2	3	4	5
1	1.000000	5.000000	7.000000	7.000000	9.000000
2	0.200000	1.000000	5.000000	7.000000	7.000000
3	0.142857	0.200000	1.000000	1.000000	3.000000
4	0.142857	0.142857	1.000000	1.000000	3.000000
5	0.111111	0.142857	0.333333	0.333333	1.000000
Column Total	1.596825	6.485714	14.33333	16.33333	23.000000

Thus, from Table 5.1, we see that "easy to close" has a strong importance over "stays open on a hill." Since we have made this assignment, we see that when "stays open on a hill" (2 on the row) is compared to "easy to close" (1 on the column), we simply put the inverse of the original comparison in that cell. That inverse is 1/5 as shown in Table 5.2.

Once we have created this pairwise matrix of comparison of customer requirements, we are ready to apply the method of the AHP. The steps to follow are as follows:

Step 1: Obtain the column total. This is done by obtaining the sum of all the weights in each cell in a particular column. For example, for column 1, the sum is 1.596825 and for column 5, the sum is 23.

Step 2: Divide each entry in a cell by its column total. For example, the column total for "easy to close" is 1.596825. When the first entry in that

Table 5.2.
Row Average Operation

	1	2	3	4	5	Row average
1	0.626243	0.770925	0.488372	0.428571	0.391304	0.541083
2	0.125249	0.154185	0.348837	0.428571	0.304348	0.272238
3	0.089463	0.030837	0.069767	0.061224	0.130435	0.076345
4	0.089463	0.022026	0.069767	0.061224	0.130435	0.074583
5	0.069583	0.022026	0.023256	0.020408	0.043478	0.03575
						1

column which is 1 is divided by the column total of 1.596825, the value of 0.626243 shown in Table 5.3 is obtained.

Table 5.3.
Consistency Matrix Operation

Consistency Matrix						
	1	2	3	4	5	A	A/Row Average

						A	A/Row Average
1	0.541083	1.36119	0.534418	0.522083	0.321752	3.280526	6.062887
2	0.108217	0.272238	0.381727	0.522083	0.250252	1.534516	5.636671
3	0.077298	0.054448	0.076345	0.074583	0.107251	0.389925	5.107375
4	0.077298	0.038891	0.076345	0.074583	0.107251	0.374368	5.019465
5	0.06012	0.038891	0.025448	0.024861	0.03575	0.185071	5.176785
						Average	**5.400637**
						CI	**0.100159**
						CR	**0.089428**

Step 3: Obtain the row averages. These row averages are known as the priority indices. For example, the row average of 0.541 shows the relative importance of the customer requirement "easy to open." It is seen here that "easy to close" is the most important customer requirement item followed by "stays open on a hill" with a priority index of 0.272. The least important customer requirement item is "no road noise" with a priority index of 0.035. It appears that "easy to open" and "doesn't leak in rain" are of equal importance with priority indexes of 0.076 and 0.074 respectively. Thus, the QFD team should focus more attention in satisfying the customer by designing the product for "easy to close" and "stays open on hill," while the other items are of less significance.

Step 4: However, before these priority indexes can be used in a QFD framework, it is important to validate them by checking for consistency in the judgment of the QFD team. This is done by using the priority indexes generated in Table 4.2, and the original weight assignments in Table 4.1. Each column of Table 4.1 is multiplied by its corresponding priority index given as the last column of Table 4.2.

Step 5: Take the sum of the cells in each row of Table 4.3 and create a new column. This new column is labeled A. Divide each of the row sums given in column A by its associated priority index, to create column B. For example, the first entry in column B = 6.06289 as shown in Table 4.3. This entry is obtained as (The first entry in column A)/Priority index for Row 1. Which is 3.28053/0.54108.

Step 6: Take the average of the entries in the column A. Let that average be known as *L*. Therefore,

$$L = (3.28 + 1.53 + 0.38 + 0.37 + 0.18)/5 = 5.4$$

Step 7: Let CI = Consistency Index where

$$CI = (L - N)/(n - I)$$

and n = number of items being compared or the size of the pair wise comparison matrix. For this problem,

$$CI = (5.4 - 5)/(5 - 1) = 0.100159$$

Step 8: The Consistency Ratio (CR) is defined as

$$CR = CI/RI$$

where *RI* is known as random index which is the consistency index of a randomly generated pairwise comparison matrix. For this problem, $CR = 0.100159/1.12 = 0.0894$. Since this value is 0.10 or less, it is considered acceptable. We can, therefore, conclude that the QFD team is consistent in its judgment. Otherwise, we need to identify the source of the inconsistency and follow the iterative procedures provided by Madu (1994) to resolve this conflict before arriving at an acceptable priority indexes for customer requirement items. The random index is given in Table 5.4.

Now that we have validated the consistency of QFD team in obtaining the priority indexes, we can apply them in the QFD. We shall go back to Figure 4.4 and replace the "importance to customer" weights used in that problem with the 'customer priority indexes' we have just generated. Thus, we obtain Figure 5.2.

Table 5.4.
Random Index Table

N	3	4	5	6	7	8
RI	0.58	0.90	1.12	1.24	1.32	1.41

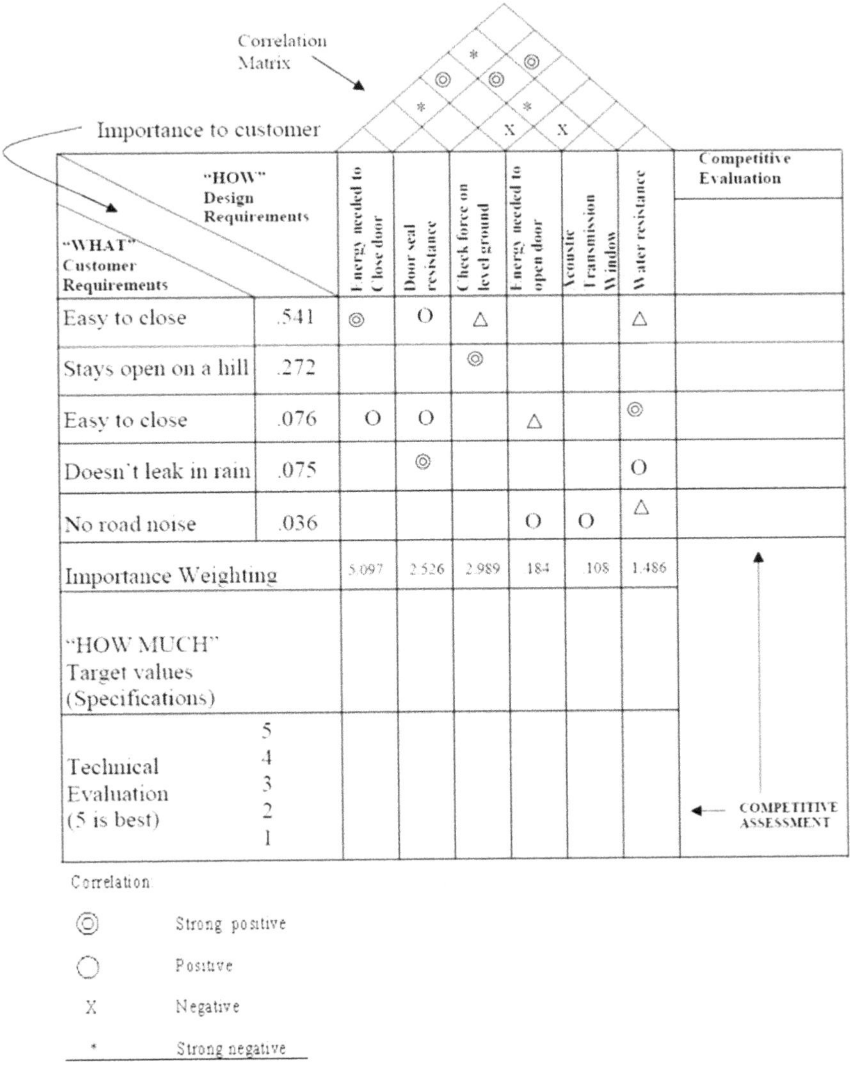

Figure 5.2. House of Quality Matrix.

Based on these new priority indices, we see that the most important design requirement should be "energy needed to close door" followed by "check force on level ground" and "door seal resistance." The least important is "acoustic transmission window." We should, however, point out that this example is for illustrative purposes only. The intent of using the AHP in this chapter is to show that it is a more structured approach and will increase the likelihood of making the correct weight assignments to customer requirement items. As seen from this example, as the weights change so will the focus on design requirements. In Figure 4.4 for example, we observe that the order of design requirements is different from the order observed in Figure 5.2. This is because the weights we assigned to the customer requirement items have changed in their magnitude of relative importance even though their order is still the same. This shows that it is very important to carefully assess the weights that are assigned to customer requirement items.

Analytic Network Process

Analytic Network Process (ANP) is a more complex extension of the Analytic Hierarchy Process and was also developed by Thomas L. Saaty (1987). Unlike the hierarchical structure assumed in the AHP, ANP allows for interrelationships or interdependence between the different levels as in the structure of AHP and also allows internal dependence. As a result, it is more versatile since it represents more closely how decisions are made in real life. However, this better representation of reality also makes it a more complex application. The ANP uses similar pairwise comparison scales that were used in AHP. Figure 5.1 shows the difference between AHP and ANP. Notice that AHP is strictly hierarchical while ANP allows for inner dependence which is shown with a loop and outer dependence which is represented with an arrow. The ANP application to QFD has been illustrated in several publications (Abastante & Lami, 2012; Colochia, 2001; Lesmes, Castillo, & Zarama, 2009; Singh & Kumar, 2014). We shall briefly describe a simple network as shown in Figure 5.1 since the mathematical computation is outside the scope of this book and will also require the use of a specialized software.

Step 1: Model Structure

In a "simple" network case, there may be interdependence among the components, criteria and alternatives that are presented as the different hierarchies in an AHP (de Steiguer, Duberstein, & Lopes, 2003)

Furthermore, components may also belong to clusters. ANP also allows for feedbacks and loops. These interrelationships can be used to form a network structure. While the AHP shows a unidirectional hierarchical relationship, the ANP shows that the different decision levels may be inter-related. This relationship could be between different levels of hierarchy (outer dependence) or within the elements in the same component (inner dependence). The arrows that are used to show the interdependence between the different components can be either unidirectional or bidirectional to show the direction of the dependence.

Step 2: Construct Pairwise Comparison Matrix and Find the Relative Weights

Once the relationships are established, the different pairwise comparison matrices can be established. The standard approach of AHP can be used both in constructing the pairwise comparison matrices and in determining the relative weights of the elements. The consistency ratio can also be obtained to guide the rationality of the decision-making process.

Step 3: Build Super Matrices

The steps discussed onwards, distinguish ANP from AHP. The super matrix takes the following forms:

a. An initial un-weighted super-matrix is developed. This is a bigger matrix used to obtain global priorities for a network that has interdependent influences. It is a partitioned matrix with each matrix segment representing the relationship between two nodes (i.e., components or decision levels). The priorities obtained in Step 2 above are also included in the matrix at the appropriate location of the matrix as local priority vectors and will show the interdependence between the components or elements within the same component.

b. The super-matrix is then weighted to make it stochastic. This is done by multiplying the un-weighted super-matrix by the weight obtained for each component or cluster. A cluster can consist of the grouping of more than one component as a cluster. When the columns of the matrix become stochastic, they sum up to 1.00. The super-matrix will now be able to converge when its limit is taken by raising it to an arbitrary large number. The values obtained in the limit super-matrix will become stable. The values obtained will represent the global priority of each element of the network.

c.   The limit super-matrix is obtained by raising the matrix obtained in (b) to a very large number to yield long-term weights that are now relatively stable. Usually, the matrix is raised to the power $2k + 1$ where k is an arbitrary large number. This new matrix is known as limit super matrix. It is similar to the weighted super matrix; however, all its columns are the same after this operation is done. Once this is done, the final priorities of all the elements in the matrix can be obtained.

Step 4: Optimal Choice

The best choice can now be selected based on the higher priority index provided in the normalized matrix provided that the entire network was included in the super-matrix. Sometimes, the super-matrix may not be inclusive of all the components in the network and may simply show only interrelated components. In that situation, further calculations may be needed to compute the overall priorities before the optimal choice can be selected.

Sometimes, like in the QFD, the interest may be in developing priorities either for the customer requirements or for design requirements. Each of the customer or design requirement may involve several subcriteria and elements and they may be interdependent thus requiring that interdependent relationships are considered in order to come up with the appropriate priority indexes.

In using the ANP, we end up working with large matrices thus there is need to use computer software to solve such problems. A popular software that is being used for this model is the *Super Decisions* software. ANP has some advantages over the use of AHP. As we mentioned earlier, it models real life decision making better than AHP by allowing feedbacks and interdependencies to be considered. It is more flexible since it does not require adherence to strict hierarchical structure. It is more precise and objective. However, it is disadvantaged by the fact that it is complex, requires a lot of matrix operations which may necessitate the use of special software packages. It is also time consuming and we recommend that it is better to use it with a group of people who are knowledgeable about the QFD problem to be solved so that the right dependencies can be identified, and proper assessment of the problem made. Interested readers may refer to some of the references cited in this chapter.

Big Data and QFD

This is the era of big data. There are several data mining techniques that can be employed to both identify customer requirements and design specifications. Effective quality plan requires that we are able to match both customer requirements and design specifications. We can now discern some of the actions competitors are taking to enrich customer experiences. ANP can help to explore the interdependencies between customer requirements and design specifications. We now have the capacity to explore the complexity in this problem. With the rapid proliferation of new information and new technologies as briefly outlined in Chapter 3, data analytics methods can be employed to identify customer requirements and design specifications that can be fed into ANP. ANP can be used to prioritize them so that attention is focused on those factors that will help to enrich customer experience. In the dynamic market environment, it is important to consider the avalanche of customer and competitors' information from different sources so that the key information that affect product quality and performance can be identified. Thus, the horizon of consideration for customer requirements and design specifications should be expanded to take advantage of big data and data analytics. ANP will therefore be a valuable tool to address this complex problem and integrate the information in a QFD framework. Mazur (2014) identified some benefits of using big data to identify customer needs to include market segmentation where statistical methods can be used to identify hidden differences in demographics and use modes; and discovery of preferences based on purchases of unrelated items. Conversely, the concerns about big data relate more to methodological and security concern issues. Some of these issues are systematically being addressed as big data is becoming increasingly important.

IWM Case

AHP has been widely applied. Many systemic problems are multi-faceted in nature and can only be thoroughly solved when interacting and interdependent variables are all considered. In watershed planning, social, economic, and ecological and policy concerns play major roles in determining the best plan. Integrated Watershed Management is one of the preferred models of watershed planning. This model is capable of integrating all the multi-faceted variables that we have just listed in other to identify the best watershed plan. This is possible through the use of stakeholders whose inputs and expert knowledge of the problem are analyzed using the AHP. The AHP treats the planning criteria and their weights in an open and explicit manner. The use of stakeholders in this problem solving also helps to ensure that the important participants in this critical decision-making problem are involved and their decisions duly considered (Abastante & Lami, 2012).

CONCLUSION

In this chapter, we focused on the importance of the weights assigned to customer requirement items. We showed that these weights affect the importance weights obtained for design requirements and may therefore, affect the focus of designers in trying to satisfy customer requirements. Our recommendation is to use a structured approach such as the AHP in obtaining customer requirement priority indices. We provided a step-by-step approach to do that and we also showed how consistency in the QFD team's judgment could be tested. The final priority indices obtained was applied in a QFD context and used to resolve the problem presented in Figure 4.4. We also pointed to other benefits of using structured techniques such as the AHP especially in a group decision-making context as involved when a QFD team is assembled.

SELF STUDY QUESTIONS

1. What is AHP?
2. Why is AHP a good approach to obtain customer requirement priority indices?
3. What are some of the problems encountered while assigning weights without the use of AHP?
4. What are the steps to obtain the customer requirement priority indices? Give a case analysis on this. How would you deal with inconsistent opinions?
5. Distinguish between AHP and ANP and descriptively illustrate how they can be applied in QFD.

REFERENCES

Abastante, F., & Lami, I. (2012). Quality function deployment (QFD) and Analytic Network Process (ANP): An application to analyze a cohousing intervention. *Journal of Applied Operational Research, 4*(1), 14–27.

Colochia, I. C. (2001). Analytic network process—Decision making with dependence and feedback. Retrieved from http://my.liuc.it/MatSup/2010/N90212/_Lezione_MMAI_CC.pdf

de Steiguer, J. E., Duberstein J., & Lopes V. (2003). The Analytic Hierarchy Process as a means of integrated watershed management. Retrieved from http://scarletandminiver.com/wp-content/uploads/2016/04/de-steiguer-ahp.pdf and http://www.tucson.ars.ag.gov/icrw/Proceedings/Steiguer.pdf

Lesmes, D. L., Castillo, M., & Zarama, R. (2009). *Application of the Analytic Network Process (ANP) to establish weights in order to re-accredit a program of a university.*

Proceedings of the International Symposium on the Analytic Hierarchy Process 2009. Retrieved from http://isahp.org/2009Proceedings/Final_Papers/44_ LesmesCastilloZarama_ANPinWeightingUniversityPrograms_REV_FIN.pdf

Madu, C. N. (1994). A quality confidence procedure for GDSS application in multicriteria decision making. *IIE Transactions, 26*(3). Retrieved from https:// www.tandfonline.com/doi/abs/10.1080/07408179408966605?journalCode= uiie20

Mazur, G. (2014). *Keynote: QFD and the New Voice of Customer (VOC).* International Symposium on QFD, Istanbul, Turkey. Retrieved from http://www.mazur.net/ works/Mazur_2014_QFD_and_New_VOC.pdf

Saaty, T. L. (1987). Rank generation, preservation, and reversal in the Analytic Hierarchy Decision Process. *Decision Sciences 18*, 157–177.

Saaty, T. L. (1996). *Decision making with dependence and feedback: The Analytic Network Process.* Pittsburgh, PA: RWS. Retrieved from http://www.cs.put.poznan.pl/ ewgmcda/pdf/SaatyBook.pdf

Singh, S., & Kumar, M. (2014). Application of analytical network process in quality function deployment. International *Journal of Computer Applications (0975– 8887). National Conference on Innovations and Recent Trends in Engineering and Technology (NCIRET–2014).* Retrieved from https://pdfs.semanticscholar.org/ e084/3af642ecc07525c70d228f05c0328d15030a.pdf

CHAPTER 6

QFD AND BENCHMARKING

In Figure 4.4, we provided a competitive assessment of company X against companies A and B. This assessment is helpful in evaluating company X performance against its competitors. This chapter focuses on the integration of benchmarking in QFD. This linkage will help the QFD team to design and produce superior products and services for its customers. First, we explore the meaning and definitions of benchmarking. Chen and Paetsch (1998) provide an excellent introduction to benchmarking. The origins of benchmarking in business practices can be traced to Xerox Corporation. Xerox used benchmarking as one of its quality techniques to successfully overcome the Japanese competitive challenges in the late 1970s and the middle 1980s. Since then, several other major corporations around the world have gracefully adopted different forms of benchmarking. Notable among these companies are Ford Motor Company, AT&T, Texas Instrument, and Lexus. As benchmarking techniques have grown popular so have the definitions of benchmarking. One of the earliest definitions of benchmarking is from Xerox. As expected, benchmarking has its origins from the corporate world and most of the definitions have also come from the corporate world rather than academia. Some of the definitions are presented below.

Xerox: "continuous process of measuring our products, services and practices against our toughest competition or those companies recognized as world leaders."

Ford Motor Company: "a structured approach for learning from others and applying that knowledge."

Texas Instruments: "a quality improvement tool that enables us to measure our products, services and practices against those of our toughest competitors or other leading companies."

AT&T: "continuous process of measuring our current business operations and comparing them to best in-class companies."

3M: "tool used to search for enablers that allow a company to perform at best-in-class level in a business process."

What is clear from this is that there is no universal definition of benchmarking for business practices. Each corporation defines it as it suits its needs and goals. However, one common theme in all these definitions is the focus on learning from the best in class to improve performance. There are several other definitions of benchmarking, which reiterate most of the definitions given by business. These definitions have generally come from researchers (Grayson, 1994), Madu and Kuei (1995), and Spendolini (1992).

TYPES OF BENCHMARKING

There are four major types of benchmarking that was originally offered by Xerox. These are namely, internal, competitive, functional and generic. Internal benchmarking involves comparing similar operations within the organization. The focus is inward as a result it may not be possible to achieve the best in class since the sampling frame is limited. As Chen and Paetsh (1998), noted, the potential for improvement through internal benchmarking is modest at 10%. Competitive benchmarking on the other hand involves comparing one against its direct competitors. This is more difficult to achieve because of legal and competitive constraints. The potential for improvement is estimated at about 20%. Functional benchmarking requires comparing ones operation to similar operations in one's own industry. Functional benchmarking is considered to be easy and potential for improvement is in the 30% range. Generic benchmarking involves comparing one's function or activity to any best-in-class performer irrespective of the industry. For example, an auto manufacturer may benchmark LL Bean for its packaging even though they are in different industries. This type of benchmarking is considered easy to implement, the sampling frame is large, and potential for improvement is in the 30% range.

The classification of benchmarking provided above is often referred to as the Xerox model. The focus is more on whom to benchmark. Madu and Kuei (1995) offered an alternative classification scheme. Their scheme, which consists of five types of benchmarking, focuses on what, is to be benchmarked. This adds to the original classification by Miller, DeMeyer, and Nakane (1992). The five categories that emerge are product, functional, best practices, strategic and systemic. Chen and Paetsh (1998) recommended that the best practices could be better-renamed best management practices. The definitions are adapted from Madu and Kuei (1995).

Product benchmarking: The focus is to learn from competitive products that are the best-in-class performers. For example, when Toyota introduced its luxury Lexus cars, it had to benchmark top performers such as Mercedes and BMW. The learning gained from this process was instrumental in designing and producing competitive cars in the luxury car market.

Functional benchmarking: The focus here is on benchmarking the process rather than the product. For example, a manufacturer may be interested in learning specific production processes from recognized leaders. Such processes may include Just-in-Time, Flexible Manufacturing Systems, or Lean Production.

Best-Practices Benchmarking: Emphasis here is on management practices. Attention is given to work related matters such as the role of the work environment on performance, salary incentives, safety guidelines, and so forth. General Electric (GE) is known as a major advocate of best-practices benchmarking.

Strategic benchmarking: The emphasis here is on the overall business strategy of the organization. It is checked for consistency and compared to results derived from other benchmarking practices.

Systemic benchmarking: This goes beyond the normal business strategy to include overall organizational performance. The organization caters to the global needs of its customers by laying emphasis on environmental protection and social responsibility issues. The goal is to learn from the practices of organizations that are leaders in environmental protection and social responsibility issues.

An organization can improve its performance through the process of benchmarking. The traditional application of QFD has been in the area of product or service design. However, QFD application is being extended to a variety of organizational activities. Companies can use QFD for both their internal and external activities to identify critical activities to focus on to improve their performance. Each of the five types of benchmarking discussed above can form an object of QFD assessment by a QFD team. For example, with systemic benchmarking, a company may try to understand external needs of both internal and external customers as they relate to the natural environment and match those needs with design requirements. In fact, the company will be more competitive if it takes a holistic posture of its products and activities rather than focusing on the direct product alone. Thus, QFD can be applied not only in designing product quality but also in integrating environmental factors in the product design, improving the efficiency of production activity, and in achieving corporate social responsibility. In the next section, we shall discuss the benchmarking component of the "House of Quality" namely the competitive and the engineering evaluations.

COMPETITIVE EVALUATION

From Figure 4.4, we construct Figure 6.1, which is the competitive assessment matrix. This matrix allows the QFD team to position its product or services against that of the company's major competitors.

Customer requirements						Competitive evaluations
						$X = US$
						$A = Competitor\ A$
						$B = Competitor\ B$
						(5 is best)
	1	2	3	4	5	
Easy to close	X			AB		
Stays open on a hill			AB	X		
Easy to open		X		A	B	
Doesn't leak in rain			XB	A		
No road noise		X	B	A		

Figure 6.1.   Competitive Assessment Matrix.

The type of benchmarking employed here is product benchmarking. Company X is comparing its product against those of companies A and B identified as their major competitors. We can take each of the customer requirement items one at a time and see how well company X is doing when compared to its major competitors. First, with "easy to close," we notice that company X is doing very poorly when compared to companies

A and B. Although companies A and B are doing much better, they still need to improve on this item since none of them appears to be getting the top score of 5. Furthermore, from Figures 4.4 and 5.2, we observe that "easy to close" is the most important customer requirement. This should be a major concern to company X since it can not be competitive if it fails to satisfy this important customer requirement. Obviously, company X needs to benchmark companies A and B and then, try to surpass it on this customer requirement item by targeting to achieve a score of 5.

Next to "easy to close" in the order of importance to the customer is "stays open on a hill." Company X appears to be doing very well and much better than companies A and B. Companies A and B have comparable performance. However, company X still needs improvement to achieve the score of 5. From Figure 6.1, it is apparent also that company X trails its competitors in the remaining customer requirement items although they are of less significance as shown in Table 5.2.

Based on the information derived from this benchmarking analysis and the relative priorities assigned to customer requirement items in Table 5.2, company X should focus its resources to being the best performer in terms of "easy to close" and "stays open on a hill." Currently, it is doing better than its competitors with regards to "stays open on a hill" but could do much better. Conversely, it trails poorly with regards to "easy to close." It needs to adequately satisfy these two major customer requirements in order to be competitive. Next, we will look at the engineering evaluation.

ENGINEERING EVALUATION

Once the QFD team identifies what the customer needs, the next thing it ought to do is to find out how to satisfy those needs. Primarily, this is accomplished through incorporating the requirements into the design of the product. We have illustrated this point in Chapters 3 and 4. In these chapters also, we showed a technical evaluation chart within the "House of Quality." In this section, we shall magnify that chart and discuss the benchmarking aspect of the chart. This is presented as Figure 6.2. Notice from Figure 6.2, that there exist a significant technical gap between company X and its competitors companies A and B in almost all the design requirements. For example, company X has a rating score of 2 with respect to the 'energy needed to close door' while company A has a score of 5. Also, notice that from the importance weighting attached to the design requirements, the "energy needed to close door" is apparently, the most important design requirement needed to achieve customer satisfaction. This technical gap suggests an area that the QFD team must focus on developing sufficient capabilities in order to deliver competitive products or services that

Technical evaluation (5 is best)	Energy needed to close door	Door seal resistance	Check force on level ground	Energy needed to open door	Acoustic transmission window	Water resistance
5	A	A	BA	A		BA
4		X		B	BXA	X
3	B		X			
2	X	B		X		
1						

Figure 6.2.   Engineering Evaluation.

will meet customer needs. From Figure 4.4 and 5.2, we observe that the other three major design requirements are "door seal resistance," "check force on level ground," and "water resistance." Company X appears to have sufficient technical capacity to satisfy the design requirements for "door seal resistance" and "water resistance" but it is not the industry leader. Company A is the industry leader for both design requirements and shares this leadership role with company B in terms of "water resistance." Company X also lacks the technical capacity to 'check force on level ground.' Although it is equally comparable with companies B and A with respect to "acoustic transmission window," however, this is the least important design requirement. The engineering benchmarking chart presented in Figure 6.2 clearly shows that company X does not have the technical superiority needed to satisfy the customer requirements. It is transparent from this that the technological gap that exists between company X and its competitors must be significantly narrowed if it intends to satisfy customer needs for the product or service. If this technical gap persists, company X will not be competitive and will not survive in this business. There is an apparent need for quick learning and possibly, reengineering for company X to survive in this business.

Benchmarking as orchestrated here through QFD is important because it makes the QFD team take a critical role in its company's operations. The team comes to understand the needs of the customer and the company's lack of competitiveness. Through QFD for example, company X is able to match its strengths and weaknesses against that if its competitors. A detailed study of these strengths and weaknesses could suggest areas for continuous improvement (i.e., those areas with sufficient technical capabilities or highly competitive evaluations) and areas for reengineering (i.e., those areas with significant technical gaps). An appropriate decision may, therefore, be needed to either acquire the needed technical capacity in terms of human resources or process changes or to in fact, drop the product line if there is no feasibility for achieving the type of improvement needed to achieve customer satisfaction.

CONCLUSION

In this chapter, we discussed briefly the origins of benchmarking and the different types of benchmarking. We also illustrated with an example how bechmarking is useful in making competitive and engineering or technical evaluations in a QFD framework. Benchmarking through QFD could help the organization to identify potential weaknesses and strengths and focus its resources to close technical and competitive gaps when possible. The benchmarking information could also be useful in a decision-making environment where there may be need for either continuous improvement or re-engineering. For example, when the company has sufficient technical capacity, it does not relax. Rather, it could gradually continue to improve on its technology until their may be need for a complete overhaul. However, when there is a large technical gap, a quantum leap change or reengineering will be needed if the company intends to satisfy the customer and become competitive. Without such a rapid reaction to achieve change, the company may never catch up with its competitors let alone surpass them. This may lead to the further demise of the company or a complete withdrawal from that market. Thus, benchmarking through QFD could lead to important decision making. However, the user must be able to read the information that is being generated through this process. The benchmarking procedure discussed here can be applied at each stage of the QFD development and to any type of benchmarking discussed above.

SELF STUDY QUESTIONS

1. Why is benchmarking very helpful in making competitive, engineering or technical evaluations?
2. What are the types of benchmarking? Give a brief explanation for each of them.

REFERENCES

Chen, I. J., & Paetsch, K. A. (1998). Benchmarking: a quest for continuous improvement. In C. N. Madu (Ed.), *Handbook of total quality management*. Boston, MA: Kluwer.
Grayson, J. (1994, May). Back to the basics of benchmarking. *Quality*, pp. 20–23.
Madu, C. N., & Kuei, C.-H. (1995). Strategic total quality management. Westport, CT: Quorum Books.
Miller, J.G., DeMeyer, A. & Nakane, J. (1992). *Benchmarking global manufacturing*. Homewood, IL: Irwin.
Spendolini, M. J. (1992). *The benchmarking book*. New York, NY: AMACOM Press.

CHAPTER 7

QFD AND
STRATEGIC PLANNING

In this chapter, we discuss the fit between QFD and strategic planning. Our aim is to show that QFD is closely associated to the overall goal and survivability of the firm. QFD is the driving force behind a firm's business strategy. In the absence of a business strategy, the firm has no purpose, no focus, and cannot be in business. Yet, business strategy can not be developed without an understanding of customer needs and the firm's ability to satisfy those needs. The mere existence of a business is often related to its strategy and it is through QFD that business strategies can be made functional. This chapter will expand on this discussion and present a strategic planning framework as a guide.

Every successful business must have a strategic plan. Planning is essential in the management of any organization. As Fayol (1984) noted, planning is a means of "assessing the future and making provision for it." Radford (1980) defined planning as involving three phases: visualizing possible future situations the organization may be involved in; ordering the situations' preferences relative to the objectives of the organization; and contemplating how the most preferred future situation can be accomplished while the least preferred is avoided. There are key points that can be identified from these definitions of planning, namely the need

---

The House of Quality in a Minute:
A Guide to Quality Function Deployment (3rd Ed.), pp. 65–75
Copyright © 2020 by Information Age Publishing

to anticipate the future that the organization may be involved in and developing strategies to deal with that future. Also, the preferences to address the future situations must be ordered and made suitable to the objectives of the organization. Clearly, any meaningful organization must have a purpose or a definition for its existence. The organization must offer a product and/or service that will chart its course to the future. Without a purposeful objective, the organization is nonexistent. Once there is a purpose, there must also be demand for that purpose as may be articulated in terms of the product or service that is being offered. For example, companies that offer products or services anticipate satisfying the demands generated by customers. Governments anticipate public service. Thus, any form of organization must have a purpose, which needs to be broken down in terms of product or service offerings. Furthermore, there must be an audience for whatever service or product that is being offered. However, just having a purpose or the target audience is not enough to sustain this purposeful organization. The organization must make sure that its product or services meet a level of excellence that will guarantee customer satisfaction. Otherwise, the organization risks failure. QFD can therefore, be used as a strategic tool to help an organization chart its course. We shall now discuss the QFD from a strategic perspective. First, we present Figure 7.1, which shows three major steps to incorporating QFD into an organization's strategic plan. These three steps are Preplanning (Business Strategy), Evaluation and Action-Implementation.

As shown in this figure, there is a sequence and this sequence goes in the order presented in Figure 7.1. We first start with a business strategy for evaluation and then action-implementation. Furthermore, the loops that are shown in this Figure imply that this is an open system that receives feedback through each stage of the process. The feedback received may redirect the QFD team to any of the precedent steps. We shall discuss each step in detail below.

QFD PARADIGM

In this section, we present a strategic framework denoted as the QFD paradigm. The QFD paradigm is a way of thinking through the business strategy of the firm by breaking down the mission to that of satisfying customer needs and showing how this could be done through the methods of quality function deployment.

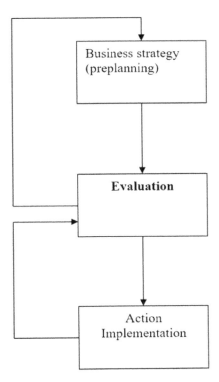

Figure 7.1. Business Strategy Paradigm.

BUSINESS STRATEGY PARADIGM (PREPLANNING)

The business strategy paradigm starts by identifying the broad mission, vision, goals and objectives of the organization. This paradigm will address how management views the organization and outline the organization's boundaries. It is through this doctrine that the mission of the organization can be understood by its members and effectively achieved. Business strategy paradigms must be based on a vision of the firm. The organization must have an understanding of its present position in the industry and where it wants to be in the future and how it intends to get there. Visionary leaders can develop an effective business strategy paradigm that can guide the organization to a promising future. Once the business strategy is developed, it must be frequently evaluated to align it with the dynamic changes in the environment. Companies like Harley-Davidson, Inc., Xerox, and US auto manufacturers all underwent paradigm shifts in the 1970s and 80s to realign their business strategies to focus on product quality.

This shift helped them to regain lost market shares and compete effectively with Japanese companies. One key factor in any business strategy is that it always contains an element of trying to satisfy the customer or winning the confidence of the customer. This cannot be done without a breaking down of a business strategy into tactical or operational terms that can be achieved by all units within the organization. The QFD team serves that role as it is made of members of the cross-functional units of the organization. The inter-functional nature of the QFD team makes it possible to identify and understand the different worldviews of the different departments, resolve emerging conflicts that may hinder the ability to achieve organizational goals, and optimize the resources of the organization to achieve a common goal. Through this, redundant activities could be eliminated, optimization rather than sub-optimization will be achieved, and the business of satisfying the customer becomes the business of all functional units within the organization and not just that of the marketing or salespeople. Designers are therefore, not afar from the end users. Designers no longer have to offer the customer the product as they see it. Rather, they offer the customer the product as the customer sees it.

Once the missions of the organization are laid out, and the business it is in is spelled out, it is important to identify the product or service features that must be present to satisfy the customer. This is the process of listening to the voice of the customer as we laid out in Chapter 2. Through this process, a list of customer requirements can be identified. We have discussed that it is more important to focus on the significant requirements of the customer rather than on a broad list that may add little or no value to the product or service.

The QFD team must now identify the design requirements to satisfy customer needs. This is more like forming a solution strategy. The list of customer requirements ("whats") offers the problems that the organization must confront to be competitive. However, the design requirements ("hows") show how these problems may be solved. Without knowing the solution techniques, it may not be possible to satisfy customer requirements. Again, this list should focus on relevance. The most significant design requirements should be focused on. As shown, when design requirements are laid out, certain correlations may be observed and there may be need for trade-offs.

With both the customer and design requirements identified, it is important to assign target requirements for the design requirements. These target requirements are often specific, measurable and attainable. Priorities should also be established on the customer requirement items to guide the team in ensuring that those critical customer requirements are satisfied.

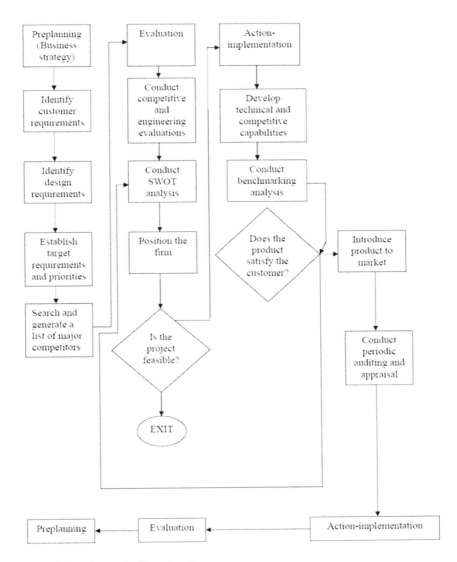

Figure 7.2. Strategic Planning Process.

These steps are outlined in Figure 7.2. As shown, the next step would be to make a list of major competitors in that product or service line. Again, the aim should be to focus on the key competitors that control a substantial share of the market. It serves no purpose to list all potential competitors who may not have any impact on the market.

EVALUATION

The evaluation phase of this process involves conducting competitive and engineering or technical evaluations. This is a process of benchmarking. Here, the organization tries to position itself against its major competitors. This will help the organization fulfill a major organizational mission. For example, where does the organization want to be? And does the organization have the resources needed to take it there? These questions can only be effectively answered if the organization understands where its competitors are and knows how to compete against its competitors for those product or service attributes that are important to the customer. With an understanding of its position in relation to its major competitors, the firm can now conduct a SWOT (strength, weaknesses, opportunities, and threats) analysis. For example, does the organization have the technical capacity? Can it develop needed technical capacity in a reasonable time? Does the organization fare well in the major customer attributes or design requirements against its competitors? By answering such questions, the firm can better position itself and judge the viability of the project. If it is deemed that it is unrealistic to attain a competitive posture in that product or service line, it may be time to exit. Otherwise, the needed technical and competitive capabilities should be developed. A new design plan should be offered that is internally checked for consistency given design parameters and customer requirements.

ACTION-IMPLEMENTATION

This phase will involve sample test marketing. The aim here is to collect information for the purpose benchmarking. Adequate statistical sample should be collected to see if the product satisfies customer requirements, and how it competes against competitors' products or services. When the QFD team is satisfied that this product or service can be competitive, it could then be introduced in a large scale to the market. The introduction of the product is not the end of the process. The product needs to be periodically reviewed and compared against other competitive products, gradual changes in product design may be necessitated overtime to add more value to the product, and information should be continuously collected from the customer to improve product or service quality. "What if analysis" should be frequently conducted to understand the perceptions of the customer when certain product features are either added, enhanced or removed. Knowledge of the market will help determine the right time to replace the product with a newer and more improved product. Information that will be obtained on on-time basis will help the firm continue to produce the product that will meet customer expectations. Notice that Figure 7.2 has a cyclic loop to denote again that this system is open and can be modified with new information.

QFD RELEVANCE TREE DIAGRAM

We can summarize the content of Figure 7.2 into a QFD Relevance Tree Diagram shown as Figure 7.3.

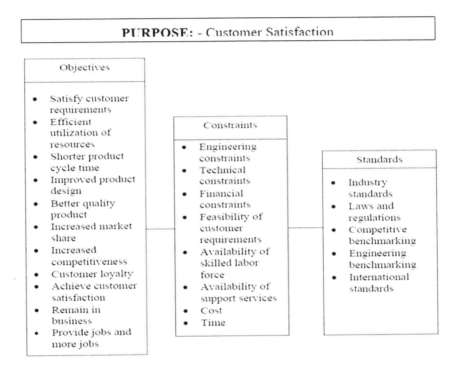

Figure 7.3. QFD Relevance Tree Diagram.

Figure 7.3 shows that the mission and purpose of the organization is to achieve customer satisfaction. This mission is worthwhile since the survival of the organization is directly related to its ability to satisfy and retain its customers. However, this mission can be achieved if certain objectives are satisfied. These objectives include providing products and services that satisfy customer requirements, making efficient use of resources, developing shorter product cycle times, improving product design and quality, and so forth. While these objectives may lead to achieving the mission, they may not all be easily attainable. Certain constraints may limit the ability to achieve these objectives. Such constraints may include time—if the product cannot be introduced timely to regain competitiveness; cost— the cost of introducing a competitive product may be too high; engineering and technical—lack of appropriate technology or skill may make it difficult to effectively satisfy customer requirements; human resources—properly trained human resources may not be available; support—some support services needed may not exist. These constraints must be evaluated on how they may potentially influence the organization's mission and goals and appropriate steps taken to resolve potential conflicts. It is also important to set standards. These standards will be the standards that the product or service must meet in order to be competitive. Such standards should be cognizant of industry standards as well as competitors' standards. Thus, competitive and engineering benchmarking should be undertaken in order to set these standards.

PLAN-DO-CHECK-ACT (PDCA) CYCLE

The discussions outlined in this chapter are similar to the PDCA cycle popularized by Deming. This is shown in Figure 7.4. The PDCA was also discussed briefly in Chapter 3. Madu and Kuei (1995) refer to it as the strategic cycle. Clearly, it is obvious from this discussion and Figure 7.2 in particular, that the PLAN—is initiated by identifying the business strategy of the firm. This plan articulates the mission and purpose of the firm and how it intends to achieve it. A clear purpose of a business organization will be to satisfy customer requirements through the delivery of acceptable product or service. The method to achieve this mission will be to design customer requirements into the product or service. We have shown that the QFD can help us to achieve that goal. The DO involves the actual design of the product. The product design takes into consideration customer requirements, technical feasibility, and target values or standards that may have been established. The CHECK involves a comparative analysis of the product and the design requirements with that of competitors. Benchmarking is conducted at this stage to ensure that the product competes effectively with existing products in the market. Also, test marketing is conducted after the product is produced. This involves statistical sampling surveys to compare the newly designed product or the new product with major competitor's product. Market testing of the product is limited to a statistical sample drawn from the population of potential customers for the product. Information gained through this process can be used to improve the product before its large-scale introduction to the market. The

ACT deals with the large-scale introduction to the market. This does not mark the end of the process. Information gathering is important through out the life of the product. New competitive information should always be obtained, and the product should be continuously benchmarked against leading brands. Furthermore, the QFD team should continue to listen to the voice of the customer to know when new features should be added to the product or a replacement product may be offered. In addition, the "unspoken" attributes that may add value to the product should be continuously investigated as the QFD team seeks to constantly improve the quality of the product. This is a never-ending process with the overall goal of continuously improving the quality of the product or service so that customer satisfaction can be achieved.

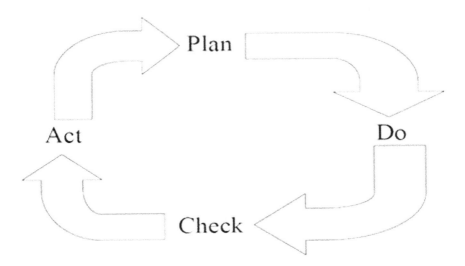

Figure 7.4. Plan-Do-Check-Act (PDCA) Cycle.

In the end, the organization is better able to deal with customer reality. The survivability of the firm rests on its ability to satisfy customer requirements. By maintaining a process that frequently monitors the product, continuously improves it by adding features that add value to the customer, the product will be able to satisfy the needs of the customer. When the product satisfies the needs of the customer, the firm becomes competitive and may gain market shares through customer loyalty. The firm will stay in business and will be able to survive and continue to offer valuable services to its customers. The QFD is indeed an important quality tool that could help guide the firm to achieve its mission.

CONCLUSION

In this chapter, we showed that the QFD is an important quality tool in achieving the strategic goals of the firm. Clearly, the purpose of business organizations is to provide quality products and services to its customers. It is only through the attainment of that goal that these businesses can survive. The QFD approach takes a strategic perspective of the business by helping the firm understand the needs of the customer and how those needs could be satisfied. It also helps the firm to position itself against its competitors so that proper decisions could be made on the direction of the firm. These decisions are based on thorough analysis of the strengths, weaknesses, opportunities and threats that the firm is confronted with. The QFD helps save organizational resources. In addition, QFD helps the organization to position itself against its competitor and be able to assess its ability to compete effectively against its competitors. We presented this discussion using a strategic framework denoted as the QFD paradigm. The QFD paradigm is a way of thinking through the business strategy of the firm by breaking down the mission to that of satisfying customer needs and showing how this could be done through the methods of quality function deployment. We have also noted that this strategic plan is similar to the PDCA cycle popularized by Deming. Finally, it is important to point the key elements of the QFD paradigm. First, it starts with a purposeful organization and must consist of three major components—planning, evaluation, and action-implementation. Second, the three phases of the QFD paradigm are inter-dependent. Third, the ability to collect timely feedback is essential to the successful use of the QFD paradigm. The use of feedback information is necessary to achieve continuous improvement in the product design and production. This paradigm operates as an open system and can receive information from its operating environment to help improve the quality of decisions that are made. Finally, the goal is to achieve customer satisfaction.

SELF STUDY QUESTIONS

1. What are the three steps to incorporate QFD into organizations strategic plan?
2. What is the QFD paradigm?
3. Plan-Do-Check-Act (PDCA) cycle has been widely used in quality management, how would you integrate it in a QFD framework?

REFERENCES

Fayol, H. (1984). *General and industrial management.* New York, NY: Institute of Electrical and Electronics Engineers.

Madu, C. N., & Kuei, C.-H. (1995). *Strategic total quality management.* Westport, CT: Quorum Books.

Radford, K. J. (1980). *Strategic planning: An analytical approach,* Reston, VA: Reston.

CHAPTER 8

QFD AND STATISTICAL QUALITY CONTROL

The ultimate goal of QFD is to produce goods and services that will meet customer requirement needs. In Chapter 7, we showed that QFD fits into the firm's strategic planning. Strategic planning deals with a broad range of issues that can be better summarized by the plan-do-check-act. In this chapter, we shall start by dissecting some sections of the planning to their operational forms. For example, how does the firm ensure that the product or service produced is meeting the pre-specified targets? For example, in Figure 3.4, one of the target values especially with respect to the major design requirement "Energy needed to close door" was "Reduce energy level to 7.5 ft/lb." This target must be measurable. Otherwise, we cannot be sure that this target value is being achieved. We also, will not be able to benchmark it against our competitors since the benchmarking phase will become entirely subjective. In this chapter, we discuss statistical quality control and how it is integrated in a QFD framework.

As we have seen so far, QFD provides a design strategy for the product or service. It does not really provide the actual production of the product or service. However, the design is like the foundation of any production process. If the design is faulty, then the production process will not have a strong foundation to stand on. And, a house without a strong foundation will eventually collapse. Ensuring that the customer's requirements are met is a multifaceted process where designing customer requirements into

The House of Quality in a Minute:
A Guide to Quality Function Deployment (3rd Ed.), pp. 77–89
Copyright © 2020 by Information Age Publishing

the product or service as provided by QFD is one aspect. For example, in a production system, the design may be sound and articulate all customer requirements however, if the incoming raw material is poor or the production process itself is incapable of meeting specifications, then customer requirements will not be satisfied. QFD as a tool works well when it is integrated with other tools that will lead to the production and delivery of quality products and services to the customer. Statistical quality control is one tool that is traditionally used for this purpose and in this chapter, we shall discuss the application. Statistical quality control comprises of two parts: acceptance sampling and statistical process control.

ACCEPTANCE SAMPLING

Acceptance sampling is normally used to test the quality of incoming raw materials or the quality of outgoing products. For example, a vendor may set a specification with the manufacturer that the "energy needed to close door" should be between 7.5 ± 0.025 ft/lb. Furthermore, in a lot of 1,000 shipments, a random sample of 100 items will be taken if 3 or more are found to be outside the specified range for the "energy needed to close the door", the entire lot will be rejected. Otherwise, it will be accepted. Notice here, that an acceptable standard has been established. This is based on the information derived from QFD that showed that this energy level would be acceptable to the customer. To ensure, that this target is met, the vendor inspects incoming lot by taking samples. These samples are usually random sample since they must represent the entire lot. If from the sample, it is detected that three or more items do not meet the standard, the entire lot (not just the sample) is rejected. This is known as acceptance sampling because, it is either that the lot is accepted or rejected. The decision to either reject or accept a lot is known as *lot sentencing*. Notice that here, we did not inspect the entire lot. Yet, we can pass judgment on the quality of the lot. The use of random sampling as we have done here has some merit. First, if the sample taken is a random sample or simple random sample, it will be a typical representation of the lot. By simple random sample, each item in the lot will have equal chance of being included in the sample. Also, the use of random sample rather than 100% inspection of the lot are very efficient. It is economical, saves time, and it is less prone to errors. Contrary to our intuition, 100% inspection does not really guarantee that more accurate decisions will be made. One major problem is that for a large population of products, it becomes almost impossible to achieve 100% inspection. Human error due to fatigue and equipment malfunction may all make it possible not to obtain reliable inspection results. In addition, there are certain products that cannot be subjected to 100% inspection. A few examples include bombs, light bulbs, and all items that may be destroyed during inspection. There are many ways to design acceptance sampling. We shall refer the reader to (Madu, 1998). We shall focus in this chapter on statistical process control since its use is common in assembly line operations. Clearly, assembly line operations may exist in either a manufacturing or service outlet. For example, banks and cafeterias to name a few use assembly line formats.

STATISTICAL PROCESS CONTROL

Statistical process control (SPC) is primarily based on the use of graphical displays known as control charts to detect shift in the process from design specifications. This is used widely for work in progress or work in process. When a shift is observed from the design specification, corrective actions are taken immediately. It could be seen that this is different from acceptance sampling since in that case, inspection is done on the finished or incoming product and not while the production process is on. The use of SPC can help to reduce waste and maximize the use of valuable resources. The objective of SPC is to improve the entire production process by ensuring that the process is on target in meeting customer requirements as identified through design requirements in QFD phase. SPC is based on the assumption that natural variation is inherent in any process. Occurrence of such variation is expected and should not be cause for alarm. For example, the target to "reduce energy level to 7.5 ft/lb." must leave room for the occurrence of natural variation. Without consideration of such variation, it may be almost impossible to achieve that target. Thus, we could specify an acceptable range within this target value by stating this specification goal as 7.5 ± 0.025 ft/lb.

Dr. Walter Shewhart introduced SPC at Bell Laboratories in the 1920s. He identified two causes of variations: common or natural causes of variation and special or assignable causes of variation. Common or natural causes of variation can be explained by chance occurrence and may not be easily controlled. For example, temperature, pressure or humidity may affect the strength of material. Product quality may be influenced by the source of the raw material. Poor process design and a poor work environment may affect the production of quality products. Some aspects of the common causes of variation may be due to the state of nature and may be inherently uncontrollable. However, there are some aspects that can be controlled. For example, the influence of poor work environment on the production of quality goods and services can be controlled. Likewise, the influence of poor incoming raw material on the quality of the finished product can be controlled. However, the authority to exert control on common causes of variation rests with top management. The production worker on the assembly floor has no control over these issues and lacks the authority to effect a change. The tools he or she is provided to do the work limit the production worker and the lack of the right tool can affect the ability to produce quality product or service. The aim of this is to quit blaming the production worker for all the problems with the product. A more holistic orientation should be resorted in order to identify the source of the problem. Obviously, management can effect a change by changing suppliers or replacing poorly designed processes.

Conversely, the operator is responsible for the special or assignable causes of variation. Such variation may occur because the operator is not properly trained and therefore, does not have the necessary skill to do the job, operator error along the production line, and so forth. Operators can do something to remove the occurrence of assignable causes of variation. They may need to get better training, or develop the skills needed to operate effectively. Statistical process control identifies only assignable causes of variation so those operators can take corrective actions. When the only variation observed is natural, then, the process is said to be stable and operating under statistical control. The process is predictable when it is stable. It will then satisfy customer requirements and meet customer expectations. Statistical control charts as presented below, are therefore, used to detect when a process is out of control.

TYPES OF MEASUREMENT

Before we discuss the control charts, we shall mention that there are two types of measurements in quality control: measurement by attributes and measurement by variables. *Measurement by attributes* is applicable when the product or service characteristic of interest is discrete or can be categorically stated. For example, suppose we go back to the specifications in Figure 3.4 and we take the specification for "Door seal resistance." Our focus may be to check if the specification is being maintained. Here, the specification is to "Maintain current level." When a sample is inspected, we may simply check "yes" if the current level is maintained and "no" if it is not maintained. Other classifications include "accept" or "reject," 0 or 1, win or lose, and so forth. When the quality characteristic of a product or service can be assessed in a categorical form as this, we have measurement by attributes. *Measurement by variables* on the other hand, deals with a situation where the quality characteristic of the product is expressed in a continuous scale. For example, the energy level needed to open or close the door is given as 7.5 ± 0.025 ft/lb. Normally, when the measurement scale is expressed in a continuous scale such as weight, height, time, temperature, length, and so forth, it is better to use measurement by variables. Measurement by variables provides more information than measurement by attributes. As a result, measurement by variables will be more powerful than measurement by attributes.

We shall use the example given in Figure 3.4 and provide one example for each measurement types and a general discussion on the use of control charts.

CONTROL CHARTS

As we mentioned at the beginning of this chapter, control charts are graph-ical displays that are used to detect shifts from design specifications. These shifts may be due to special or assignable causes of variation. The aim is to enable operators to take corrective actions while the process is ongoing. Such actions will aim to bring the process back to conformance. Standard control charts will normally have three horizontal lines namely the lower control limit (LCL), the centerline which will be the process mean, and the upper control limit (UCL). Measurements are then taken from the process and plotted on the charts as shown with dots in Figure 8.1. Points that may fall outside the LCL and the UCL may indicate non-conformance with design specification. Conversely, points that fall within the LCL and UCL may indicate conformance with design specifications.

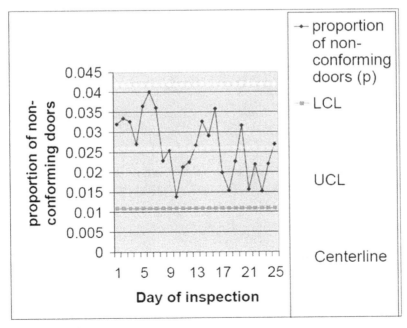

Figure 8.1. *p*-chart.

The construction of the control chart is based on statistical principles. It is assumed that the natural variations observed from a process can be explained by the normal probability distribution. As a result, it is important to have a high probability that samples taken from the process will fall within the control limits. The standard practice in establishing control limits is to set it at $\pm$ 3 standard deviations of the mean. This will imply that 99.7% of the process output is expected to fall within the control limits while only 0.3% of the process output is expected to fall outside the control limit when the process is stable or in statistical control. We shall now present the examples for each measurement type.

STATISTICAL PROCESS CONTROL CHARTS FOR ATTRIBUTES

We shall discuss the use of the p-chart as a statistical process control chart for attributes. The p-chart is applicable when it is important to investigate the proportion or fraction of non-conforming items. In our case, we investigated the proportion of non-conforming doors. That is, the proportions of doors that may not maintain the current level for door seal resistance. From Table 8.1 for example, we observe that on Day 1, 1,000 doors were inspected and 32 of them did not maintain the current level for door seal resistance. This gives a proportion of 0.032. Any time we are interested in the fraction or proportion of defective items, the p-chart will be applicable as a control chart. There are other types of control charts for attributes such as the c-chart, np-chart, and the u-chart. These charts are all somewhat related. We shall refer the reader again to Madu (1998). We shall however, focus on the p-chart. We define the proportion (p) as follows:

$$\bar{p} = \frac{\text{Total number of non} - \text{confor} \min g \text{ doors}}{\text{Total number doors inspected}} \tag{8.1}$$

We shall refer to this as the centerline. Using the centerline, which is the average, the control limits can be established as follows:

$$LCL \quad (p) = \bar{p} - 3 * \left[\sqrt{\frac{\bar{p}(1 - \bar{p})}{n}} \right] \tag{8.2}$$

$$UCL \quad (p) = \bar{p} + 3 * \left[\sqrt{\frac{\bar{p}(1 - \bar{p})}{n}} \right] \tag{8.3}$$

Table 8.1.
Proportion on Non-Conforming Doors

Day number	Number of doors inspected	Number of non-conformir doors	Proportion of non-conforming doors (p)
1	1000	45	0.045
2	985	33	0.034
3	889	29	0.033
4	925	25	0.027
5	1013	37	0.037
6	998	40	0.040
7	1025	45	0.044
8	875	20	0.023
9	980	25	0.026
10	1010	14	0.014
11	988	21	0.021
12	1022	23	0.023
13	864	23	0.027
14	920	30	0.033
15	965	28	0.029
16	1005	36	0.036
17	855	17	0.020
18	976	15	0.015
19	970	22	0.023
20	1012	32	0.032
21	958	15	0.016
22	1005	22	0.022
23	988	15	0.015
24	1000	22	0.022
25	892	24	0.027
Total	24120	658	0.680
Averages	964.8	26.32	0.027

Note also that if there is a target p value, that target value will replace the $\bar{p}$ obtained from equation (8.1) as the centerline. We shall illustrate with an example. In the case considered here, the interest is to find the proportion of doors that did not maintain the current level for door seal resistance. From Table 8.1, we observe the record of 25 days of inspection. On the average, the proportion of non-conforming doors is 0.026 over the 25-day period. Using equations (8.2) and (8.3), the LCL and the UCL are obtained as 0.011 and 0.042 respectively for the proportion of non-conforming doors. This computation is shown below Table 8.1.

Figure 8.1 presented above is indeed, the *p*-control chart for this problem. Now, let us look at that chart. It is seen that all the proportion of non-conforming doors fall within the control limits, However, we notice that on Day 6, the proportion of non-conforming doors seem to be very close to the UCL. Naturally, we will prefer a situation where the proportion of non-conforming doors is closer to zero. Notice also, that in computing the LCL, it is possible to obtain a negative value for LCL. When that occurs, we set the LCL to zero. Also, in our computation, we used the average sample size of 964.8 since the number of doors inspected varies from day to day. If the same number is inspected each day, we can simply use that number since its average will also be n. In analyzing the p-chart of Figure 8.1, we observe that all the points fall within the control limits. We may, therefore, conclude that the process is stable or operating within statistical control. Therefore, the variations we observed from day to day about the proportion of non-conforming doors are normal and can be explained by chance. When we observe out-of-control points, we try to understand the cause and the source of the variation so that the process can be corrected and brought to conformance.

STATISTICAL PROCESS CONTROL CHARTS FOR VARIABLES

We will now look at one of the most popular control charts ($\overline{X}$ and R charts). The $\overline{X}$ and R charts are based on the sample means and ranges of subgroups of samples to detect process precision and accuracy. The sample mean is used to measure accuracy or process's central location and the range measures the precision or process variability. The range rather than the standard deviation provides timely field information on the variability of the process. The subgroup size is normally kept small say less than five. When the subgroup size is large say ($n > 10$), it is preferable to use the standard deviation to compute the control limits.

In this section, we take samples of four each time to inspect the energy level to close door. The energy level needed to close door is measured in ft/lb. The target level desired is 7.5 ft/lb. The samples obtained after a 20 day-operation are contained in Table 8.2.

Table 8.2.
Samples on Energy Level to Open door (ft/lb)

Sample number	1	2	3	4 X	Average R	Range R	UCL	LCL	Range mean	UCL	LCL	Centerline	X-bar
1	7.49	7.52	7.45	7.56	7.505	0.11	0.16	0	0.071	7.55	7.45	7.50	7.51
2	7.48	7.59	7.55	7.51	7.5325	0.11	0.16	0	0.071	7.55	7.45	7.50	7.53
3	7.5	7.42	7.48	7.5	7.475	0.08	0.16	0	0.071	7.55	7.45	7.50	7.48
4	7.53	7.45	7.58	7.49	7.5125	0.13	0.16	0	0.071	7.55	7.45	7.50	7.51
5	7.49	7.51	7.56	7.45	7.5025	0.11	0.16	0	0.071	7.55	7.45	7.50	7.50
6	7.46	7.53	7.55	7.49	7.5075	0.09	0.16	0	0.071	7.55	7.45	7.50	7.51
7	7.45	7.52	7.52	7.56	7.5125	0.11	0.16	0	0.071	7.55	7.45	7.50	7.51
8	7.48	7.55	7.48	7.53	7.51	0.07	0.16	0	0.071	7.55	7.45	7.50	7.51
9	7.52	7.51	7.55	7.5	7.52	0.05	0.16	0	0.071	7.55	7.45	7.50	7.52
10	7.44	7.48	7.49	7.47	7.47	0.05	0.16	0	0.071	7.55	7.45	7.50	7.47
11	7.5	7.51	7.5	7.52	7.5075	0.02	0.16	0	0.071	7.55	7.45	7.50	7.51
12	7.59	7.5	7.49	7.52	7.525	0.1	0.16	0	0.071	7.55	7.45	7.50	7.53
13	7.52	7.49	7.55	7.49	7.5125	0.06	0.16	0	0.071	7.55	7.45	7.50	7.51
14	7.52	7.51	7.55	7.51	7.5225	0.04	0.16	0	0.071	7.55	7.45	7.50	7.52
15	7.49	7.5	7.5	7.52	7.5025	0.03	0.16	0	0.071	7.55	7.45	7.50	7.50
16	7.55	7.5	7.55	7.56	7.54	0.06	0.16	0	0.071	7.55	7.45	7.50	7.54
17	7.52	7.52	7.5	7.54	7.52	0.04	0.16	0	0.071	7.55	7.45	7.50	7.52
18	7.53	7.55	7.5	7.51	7.5225	0.05	0.16	0	0.071	7.55	7.45	7.50	7.52
19	7.53	7.5	7.49	7.5	7.505	0.04	0.16	0	0.071	7.55	7.45	7.50	7.51
20	7.51	7.49	7.51	7.56	7.5175	0.07	0.16	0	0.071	7.55	7.45	7.50	7.52
Average					7.511125	0.071	0.16						

We need to establish the control limits and develop a control chart for this problem. The control limits are defined as follows first for the $\overline{X}$ chart:

$$LCL = \overline{\overline{X}} - A2\,\overline{R} \tag{8.4}$$

$$UCL = \overline{\overline{X}} + A2\,\overline{R} \tag{8.5}$$

And for the R chart, we obtain

$$LCL = D3\,\overline{R} \tag{8.6}$$

$$UCL = D4\,\overline{R} \tag{8.7}$$

The terms A2, D3, and D4 are obtained from the Table and are reprinted here as Table 8.3.

Table 8.3.
Factors for Computing Control Charts Limits

Sample Size, n	Mean Factor, A_2	Upper Range, D_4	Lower Range, D_3
2	1.880	3.268	0
3	1.023	2.574	0
4	0.729	2.282	0
5	0.577	2.114	0
6	0.483	2.004	0
7	0.419	1.924	0.076
8	0.373	1.864	0.136
9	0.337	1.816	0.184
10	0.308	1.777	0.223

Source: Abbreviated from Special Technical Publications 15-C, "Quality Control of Materials," pp. 63 and 72, 1951, America Society for Testing Materials.

First, we shall present the steps to develop the $\overline{X}$ and R charts as provided in Madu (1998, p. 556).

- Compute the sample means for each subgroup;
- Compute the range of each subgroup;
- Compute the mean of all the subgroups. That mean is the grand mean and it is the centerline for the X chart;

- Compute the mean of all the subgroups range. That overall mean is the centerline for the R chart;
- Compute the control limits for R and plot them with the centerline;
- Plot the subgroup's individual R values on the same chart with the centerline and the control limits;
- If no out-of-control points are present in the R chart, then process precision is stable. Otherwise, identify the reasons for variation and take corrective actions;
- When the process precision is stable, construct the X chart using the centerline and control limits found above;
- Plot the subgroup's respective means on the X chart and check if the process is stable or whether corrective action should be taken.

Following these steps, we see from the R-chart given as Figure 8.2, that all the range points for the 20 subgroups fall within the control limits. Therefore, the process precision is stable. Once this is achieved, we proceed to evaluate the process accuracy in targeting an energy level of 7.5 ft/lb.

Figure 8.2 shows that all the points for the 20 subgroups fall within the control limits. Therefore, the process accuracy is stable. Thus, the process is meeting the target of 7.5 ft/lb. for the energy needed to close door. We can now, conclude that the process is stable.

INTERPRETATION OF CONTROL CHARTS

Our discussion of the control charts tend to suggest that once the sample points fall within the control limits, the process will be stable. However, the process will be unstable when the sample points fall outside the control limits. While this is generally true, it is possible for the sample points to fall within the control limits and yet, the process will be unstable. Thus, even an apparently stable process should be carefully evaluated. The following indicators of out-of-control process should be checked as outlined in Madu (1998, p. 561).

Are successive sample points below or above the centerline for say six or more samples? This could be explained by problems such as equipment malfunction, work schedule changes, material or operator differences. The sources of variation should be identified and explained to achieve a stable process.

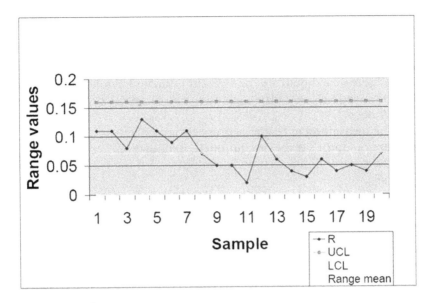

Figure 8.2. *R*-chart.

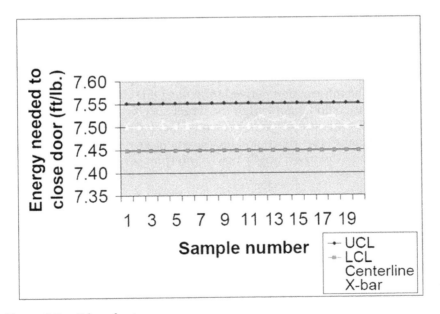

Figure 8.3. *X*-bar chart.

Does there appear to be a trend? When there is a pattern, such may indicate an out-of-control process even when it may appear as if the process is stable.

Like in the cases where we may observe a stable process, an out-of-control observance should also be carefully evaluated. Some questions need to be addressed before a firm conclusion can be reached. Such questions may include:

Are the measurement readings properly recorded?

Is there operator's error or equipment malfunction?

Are the control limits accurately computed and the control charts free of errors?

The potential sources of errors should be investigated before the problem is blamed on the process. This will help to effectively utilize time and energy in solving process problems.

CONCLUSION

In this chapter, we have developed a link between QFD and statistical quality control. We showed that while the focus of QFD is in designing products and services to meet customer requirements, that ultimately, statistical quality control principles will be applied to ensure that those requirements are designed into the product. We identified acceptance sampling and statistical process control as components of statistical quality control. However, we focused our discussion on statistical process control since it deals with work-in-process or work-in-progress. We again, illustrated with the information derived from our QFD chart (Figure 3.4) how control charts could be applied to the target specifications for the design requirements. The control charts presented focused on the use of measurement by attributes (p – chart) and measurement by variables (R and X-bar charts). We also discussed briefly how to interpret control charts.

SELF STUDY QUESTIONS

1. What are the two parts of Statistical Process Control?
2. SPC uses graphical displays known as control charts to detect shift in process. Such shifts may show instability in the process. Define a process of interest to you and determine the type of control chart you should use to check for the stability of the process. Be sure to define the type of measurement for your process before selecting a control chart.

3. What are the two causes of variations as identified by Dr. Walter Shewhart? Which is the one identified by SPC?
4. What are the two types of measurements in quality control?
5. SPC charts for variables like X-bar and R charts detect process accuracy and precision respectively. They suggest that once sample points fall within control limits the process is stable. What are some indicators to check for out-of-control process despite the sample points falling within control limits?

REFERENCE

Madu, C. N. (1998). Statistical quality control. In C. N. Madu (Ed.), *Handbook of total quality management*. Boston, MA: Kluwer.

CHAPTER 9

SIX SIGMA AND QFD

In order for today's companies to respond proactively to the needs of customers, it is imperative that processes are aligned to customer requirements and that such requirements are timely satisfied. Companies compete on several fronts, but product quality is given and must be measurable. Six Sigma is a rigorous approach to achieving quality and relies on effective data management and statistical application. The goal of Six Sigma is to apply statistics to data to identify sources of process or product defects, reduce variability, and achieve near perfection by aiming for zero defect. Conceptually, Six Sigma implies about 3.4 defects per million parts produced. Thus, quality is measurable, and zero defects can potentially be achieved since this low number is proportionally zero. Six Sigma offers a systemic and a systematic approach to identifying product or process problems by helping organizations to study their processes and workflows and enabling them to understand areas that need improvement. Effective and intelligent decisions can be made through the application of Six Sigma concept. In order to effectively analyze business processes, Six Sigma uses a five-stage approach that is referred to as DMAIC. DMAIC stands for **D**efine, **M**easure, **A**nalyze, **I**mprove, and **C**ontrol. These stages are briefly discussed.

Define—It is important for organizations to be clear on the opportunities they are faced with. Foremost in the Six Sigma approach is to define the aim or goal of the improvement activity. What is it that the organization

The House of Quality in a Minute:
A Guide to Quality Function Deployment (3rd Ed.), pp. 91–104
Copyright © 2020 by Information Age Publishing
All rights of reproduction in any form reserved.

really wants to improve on? A strategic objective may be to increase market share, reduce operating cost, achieve higher rate of return.

Measure—Measurement is essential in knowing when an objective has been achieved. Therefore, there is a need to establish reliable metrics or measurement scales to ensure that the defined objectives are being monitored. How does the organization know when higher rate of return has been achieved or when market share has been substantially increased? There needs to be a yardstick for measurement.

Analyze—From measurement, we know the current status of the process or system. We can identify the gap between the current system state and the goal, and the objective is to minimize this gap so that the goal can be achieved.

Improve—The process of improvement assumes that one understands the problems and the need to improve. Improvement requires finding better and more effective ways to do things and requires monitoring the new ways to ensure that indeed improvement was achieved.

Control—Control provides a systematic way of institutionalizing an improved system to ensure that what works is put in place. Effective standards may be applied as a way of monitoring the system's performance so that it could be effectively tracked and deviations from established standards detected on a timely basis. The control, however, is not close-looped but open to information and feedback that can be used to continuously improve and adapt the system. This way, the goal of zero defects can be effectively achieved.

Six Sigma application relies heavily on the application of statistical techniques (after all, it is a statistical concept) and management. Therefore, it should be noted that a lot of statistical tools are used in the five stages of Six Sigma. Management is also key in effective application of Six Sigma. Management of people, product, and processes are essential. When Six Sigma is effectively implemented, organizations can consistently achieve their targets, improve their performance, reduce product and process variation, and satisfy the needs and wants of customers. The ultimate result of all these will be increase in profitability, lower defects and high quality, higher employee morale, and increased competitiveness.

MEASUREMENT ISSUES IN SIX SIGMA

The aim of Six Sigma is to achieve process improvement. As we already mentioned, this is done by using a combination of statistical and management tools. By improving the sigma level, customer requirements can be achieved. The use of DMAIC that is outlined above is to enable a systematic approach to focus on measures that are "critical to quality." These measures are often referred to as CTQ for short. Six Sigma can be applied to both physical and non-physical items as may be apparent in the ever-growing service industry. While for physical items, process performance is measured in defective parts per million (ppm), for non-physical items, it is measured in terms of defects per million opportunities (dpmo). When there is less variation in the process, or the process becomes more stable and consistent, smaller deviations are achieved. Smaller deviations imply higher sigma level. Figure 9.1 presents a conversion between dpmo and sigma level.

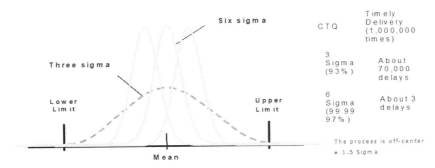

Figure 9.1.   Three Sigma vs. Six Sigma.

The customer focus adopted by Six Sigma shows that it actually works hand in hand with quality function deployment. While quality function deployment aims to design products and services that satisfy customer requirements, Six Sigma aims to achieve perfection in those products and services by reducing the variation that may exist through process improvement. In fact, the statistical and management techniques that are used to achieve Six Sigma include quality function deployment, failure mode and effect analysis, design of experiments, robust design, mistake proofing such as Poke Yoke and statistical process control (Goh & Xie, 2004). Six Sigma is an integral part of the product and service design stages. These techniques that are listed are considered at the designing stage and at the monitoring stages of the product and services. They are not end of the line application techniques. As a result, Goh and Xie (2004) note that the statistical thinking involved in Six Sigma helps to make decisions that are based on facts. Six Sigma relies on information gathering, and application of proven techniques to achieve process improvement. Finally, Goh and Xie characterized Six Sigma using "5W+1H." Specifically, this definition outlines the process of Six Sigma and how it leads to process improvement. They are adopted from Goh and Xie (2004), and Kuei and Madu (2003) and presented as follows:

1. WHY Six Sigma? Satisfaction of customers.
2. WHO does it? Structured top-down hierarchy or trained personnel.
3. WHAT is it? Statistical thinking using data to combat process variation.
4. WHERE is it? Standardized framework of "DMAIC."
5. HOW is it done? Software packages for information analysis.
6. WHEN is it done? Sustained effort via projects.

APPROACHES FOR SIX SIGMA PROJECTS

There are basically two approaches to implementing Six Sigma. We have already discussed DMAIC, which aims to achieve continuous improvement through reduction in variability of products or processes. One argument against this approach is that it may not react readily to changes. Thus, continuous improvement on a process that is out of date will not enable the organization to compete effectively. Sometimes, breakthrough thinking is needed. A popular example is the attempt to continue to improve on Polaroid instant camera when digital photography has made instant camera obsolete. The same applies in trying to improve a product that has passed its product lifecycle. Ultimately, it is important to understand what the customer wants as we have said many times in this book and then try to design Six Sigma quality into the product or process. So, the application of DMAIC will be satisfactory provided that the product or process remains capable of satisfying customer needs. Its application is not innovative but aims at eliminating or avoiding defects from an existing product or process. Once the product or process is out of favor, applying DMAIC will not help the organization to become competitive. A new strategy must be adopted. That strategy is the second approach, which is referred to as DMADV (design-measure-analyze-design-verify) or IDOV (identify-design-optimize-verify). Thus, while DMAIC achieves incremental improvement as in continuous improvement, DMADV or IDOV adopts a more radical approach and adopts the reengineering of the process. This radical approach is also often referred to as design for Six Sigma (DFSS). Harry and Schroeder (2000) claim that once organizations have reached five sigma quality levels (i.e., 233 defects per million opportunities), they need to design for Six Sigma to surpass the five sigma. As noted by Banuelas and Antony (2004), there are not enough data to substantiate the claim even though some authors have supported it. We adapt from Nave (2002) and Harry and Shroeder (2000) the assumptions made by DMAIC and IDOV as presented in Table 9.1.

Table 9.1.
Contrast of DMAIC and IDOV or DMADV

Dimension	DMAIC	IDOV or DMADV
Objective	Adopts current product or process design as correct and economical and aims to minimize the variation.	Aims to achieve resource efficiency through design to satisfy current customer and market requirements.
Process capability	Current product or process design is capable of satisfying customer needs.	Aims to achieve more than five sigma quality by producing higher yields regardless of complexity and volume.
Design	Customer needs and market requirements are satisfied by the current product configuration.	Focuses on "robustness" and capable of withstanding adverse conditions.
Flexibility	Customer needs are currently met with current configuration and design.	Has a high focus on customer demands and adapts to such demands.

Thus, the main distinction between these two approaches is the fact that DMAIC accepts the existing state of the system and works on improving it through reduction in product or process variation. Conversely, IDOV or DMADV questions the existing process and tries to develop a more proactive look by designing Six Sigma into the product or process to continually satisfy customer and market needs. It has a focus on challenges and innovation in order to meet the dynamic changes in the marketplace.

In fact, the IDOV or DMADV approach is similar to the argument proposed in Goh and Xie (2004) who countered that rather than DMAIC focusing on error or defect avoidance, that Six Sigma can be extended to include a systems perspective and strategic analysis. Systems perspective will focus on identifying appropriate system boundaries and performance indices. This will go beyond focusing on the product or process variation but to understand the macroeconomic environment that influence the "critical-to-quality" measures. The CTQs must be frequently reviewed to recognize when new measures emerge and when to adapt the list. The strategic analysis on the other hand is scenario-driven to address "what if" questions that may arise in the dynamic marketplace. Product lifecycles are short these days, technologies easily become obsolete, and customer needs and wants are fast evolving. It is important that organizations understand this dynamism and be able to react appropriately to respond to the needs of the marketplace.

SIX SIGMA AND QFD

As we have already defined, QFD is used to translate customer requirements into a set of prioritized targets that can be focused on in improving products, processes and services to satisfy the customer. These customer requirements are referred to as critical-to-quality measures in the Six Sigma literature. Six Sigma is a highly structured approach that has a strong focus on the bottom line. Achieving almost a zero defect in defects per million parts or defects per million opportunities should translate to financial gains for the organization and make the organization competitive. So, both QFD and Six Sigma aim to make the organization more competitive and successful by aligning the organization's strategy to focus on its customer and by developing means of measuring process performance improvements. One of the approaches for Six Sigma we discussed is the design for Six Sigma (DFSS). DFSS is based on listening to the voice of the customer to identify and prioritize the critical-to-quality measures that are important to the customer. These CTQs must be integrated into product and process design if the needs and wants of the customer are to be satisfied. The CTQs will be identified and prioritized by the members of the cross functional teams. This way, the organization focuses on the key CTQs and the methods of Six Sigma can be applied to achieve both robust design and minimize the variations in those key components. Indeed, with the application of QFD, Six Sigma teams can optimize their resources by targeting the CTQs that are high on importance rating to the customer. An improved process will have no value if it does not focus on what the customer wants. The customer knows what is critical to achieve his or her satisfaction. These CTQs can only be understood by listening to the voice of the customer. Thus, one can emphatically state that before Six Sigma could be applied, CTQs must be first identified and prioritized. The priorities attached to these CTQs would also influence the specification limits that should be set. The most important CTQs would definitely be set to higher specification limits such as the Six Sigma because it would be essential to significantly reduce variation in such CTQs and ensure their consistency and stability. Another aspect of the QFD is the correlation matrix, which appears as a roof in the House of Quality. By identifying potential conflicts between design requirements, emphasis is placed on the most important design requirements. Again, these become the design requirements where serious efforts must be made to achieve Six Sigma level. So, rather than the Six Sigma team using its resources to fight fires all over, it can from QFD identify both the most important customer and design requirements and focus its efforts on those. This way, a product that meets customers needs can be designed and produced on a timely fashion. Such products will also help the organization to compete effectively and become profitable.

IMPLEMENTING SIX SIGMA WITH QFD

1. The goals of Six Sigma and QFD are not quite different even though different approaches may be followed. Ultimately, the aim is to be able to satisfy customer needs so that the organization becomes competitive and profitable. To realize this goal of achieving customer satisfaction, top management participation and support are needed. Top management plays a critical role of creating and cultivating an environment that will support innovation and creativity that are essential for the implementation of QFD and Six Sigma concepts. Such an atmosphere will challenge existing hierarchical structures in the organization, division of power, and authority and breakdown the barriers that may hinder innovation and change. Top management also bears the full responsibility of allocating needed resources to ensure that the implementation of Six Sigma within QFD is successful. One area that demand resource allocation is training and the use of the best brains in the organization to effectively adapt to Six Sigma. The training requirement has often hindered the implementation of Six Sigma in smaller companies. For example, big companies like Motorola spent $170 million dollars between 1983 and 1987 on worker education that focused on quality issues such as quality improvement and designing for manufacturability. Yet, the training program must be properly designed for it to be successful. One of the early problems encountered by Motorola was that it followed a bottom up approach in its training and training lower level employees on statistical process control without providing them remedial education. When the training flopped, it was difficult to turn to top management who had not been trained to provide help. Consequently, Motorola established Motorola University to provide training to its executives. It is therefore imperative that everyone be trained, and that top management takes the lead in training. However, training does not have to be a drag on corporate resources. It is important to benchmark organizations that have efficient training programs. General Electric appears to have successful training programs that are well structured and take lesser time. For example, while it takes GE 16 to 20 weeks to train a black belt (a basic level of Six Sigma certification), it takes Motorola a minimum of one year.

2. It is important to listen to the Voice of the Customer. There must be free flow of information where customer needs and wants are identified. The critical to quality issues are known and the design strategies are developed to address such issues. Resources are efficiently utilized when it is clear which customer requirements are more

important and which design requirements need tighter specification as the Six Sigma. Thus, implementation will be more effective when the focus is on the critical design issues.

3. Training needs at the different levels of the organization must be assessed. But before the training, employees must understand the new mission of the organization to achieve customer satisfaction and how training on both QFD and Six Sigma could help realize such goals. It is important that remedial skills are provided at all levels of training to achieve both literacy and statistical understanding and must involve a top-to-bottom approach.

4. As we have mentioned above, there are two approaches to Six Sigma namely DMAIC and DMADV (or IDOV). Process implementation must involve a two-prong monitoring system. One will focus on DMAIC where incremental and continuous improvement is achieved whence the current processes and products continue to satisfy customer and market needs and the DMADV or IDOV will involve reengineering of the entire product or processes when the current system is incapable of meeting customer and market needs. This way, the organization is adopting both systemic and strategic perspectives and would be able to design for Six Sigma and adapt the design strategies as customer requirements change.

5. Cross functional teams would have to be empowered and remain actively involved in evaluating and monitoring business processes, scanning the business environment and developing strategies to continue to respond proactively to their dynamic environment.

LEAN SIX SIGMA

Many authors especially practitioners have tried to distinguish between Total Quality Management (TQM) and Six Sigma and have often confused the grey areas between the two. In fact, some distinctions have often misrepresented what TQM is in favor of the new focus on Six Sigma. While Six Sigma is in vogue in many corporations such as Motorola, GE, Seagate Technology, GlaxoSmith Kline, Ratheon, and a host of others, critics argue that Six Sigma is another management fad that may ultimately not meet the expectations of the adopting companies.

Even with the documented successes of companies like GE under the leadership of its former CEO Jack Welch, yet many companies that have tried to implement these new concepts such as TQM, Business Process Re-engineering and Six Sigma have recorded failures (Easton & Jarrell,

1998). There is also the problem of sustaining initial process improvement successes (Sherman, Keating, Oliva, Repenning, & Rockart, 1999). Further, business performance has not always improved with successes in these programs as evident with the layoffs and lack of profitability by Motorola in 1998 (Basu, 2004).

We see Six Sigma not as distinct from TQM but enabled by TQM. It could be viewed as an extension of TQM to emphasize on more structured focus on projects, performance metrics, financial returns, and structured and rigorous training on data management and analysis. Some of the critics of Six Sigma have argued that Six Sigma is a repackaging of statistical process control (SPC) which has always been encouraged in TQM applications. Edward Deming who is considered by many as the father of TQM focused a great deal on the concept of variation and the use of SPC as a necessity in order to isolate the different causes of variation: natural or assignable. However, Six Sigma is not simply an application of SPC. It also has a focus on achieving best-in-class or world class performance by targeting 3.4 defects per million parts or per million opportunities. It has a strategic focus on improving key performance metrics.

Many have even proposed Lean Six Sigma as an extension of Six Sigma. The problem of quality management is too many terms that are often pushed to be distinct when in fact, they complement each other and could be incorporated within an existing framework. Lean Six Sigma is simply an integration of Six Sigma with Lean Production. A lean organization focuses on value management and aims to eliminate nonvalue added activities. The elimination of wastes helps the organization to become more productive and efficient, and able to achieve operational excellence. Lean Six Sigma application covers the entire value delivery chain which extends to vendors and suppliers and adopts customer focus. It helps organizations to become agile and to respond rapidly to their dynamic environments.

In summary, while the distinctions between Six Sigma and TQM are often blurred, Basu (2004) identified some key foci of Six Sigma that may help delineate it from TQM. These are:

- Six Sigma has a stronger focus on statistical process control and business performance metrics.
- Training for Six Sigma is more structured with different levels of focus, rigor, and expertise.
- Six Sigma focuses on projects and the use of problem-solving techniques such as DMAIC, and DMADV or IDOV.
- Six Sigma builds its foundation on TQM.

AN EXAMPLE OF SIX SIGMA APPLICATION

In technical terms, sigma (σ) denotes variability or standard deviation of an attribute or customer requirement of interest. In statistical process control, specification limits are provided, and a critical assumption is made that the process is stable and behaving according to the normal distribution. When a process is stable, its behavior can be predicted. With the QFD phase, the customer requirements are identified and used as a basis in developing quality characteristics to measure. It is important that the process is capable of satisfying these quality characteristics in order to satisfy the needs and wants of the customer. Six Sigma helps to ensure that this is done. As we have already stated, this approach will ensure that only 3.4 defects are observed per million parts or opportunities.

There is often a misunderstanding on what the Six Sigma process means. A major assumption in the way Six Sigma concept was developed is that the shift in the process mean is within 1.5 standard deviation and that the process mean is 4.5 standard deviations from the closest specification limit and 7.5 standard deviations from the farthest specification limit. In fact, the process mean is 4.5 standard deviations from it closest specification limit and not 6 standard deviations as the term 6 sigma would tend to imply. It would probably have been better and easier to refer to this approach as "four and a half sigma" rather than "Six Sigma." Mitra (2004) provides a good description of the statistical foundation of Six Sigma and notes that the expectation that a process stays within 1.5 σ of the process may vary from process to process. In other words, each organization has to understand its process spread and mean and apply them in finding process shift.

Table 9.2 shows the basic concept of Six Sigma. If the six-sigma process is centered at the mean, then the process would produce one defective part per billion (PPB) for each specification limit or two PPB for both specification limits. Similarly, if we apply the concept that Six Sigma is 4.5 from its closest specification limit and 7.5 standard deviation from its farthest specification limit, we see that 3.4 defective parts per million (PPM) are produced. We see from Figure 9.2 when we contrast the standard 3 σ to 6 σ, that Six Sigma would tend to produce more consistent products than three sigma. Thus, the higher the number of sigma, the more capable and consistent the process becomes. A simple example would be a mail delivery company that checks its on-time delivery using three and Six Sigma respectively. A three sigma operation would expect 1,350 late deliveries per million mails and for a truly Six Sigma operation, the organization would expect two late deliveries per billion mails.

Figure 9.2 shows how the defects per part declines as organizations focus on higher sigma values. However, it should be noted that higher sigma

Table 9.2.
Computation of Defects for One-Sided Specification Limit

Z (Standard score)	Normal Probability	Complement	PPM	PPB
1	0.841344746	0.158655254	158655.3	158655253.9
1.5	0.933192799	0.066807201	66807.2	66807201.27
2	0.977249868	0.022750132	22750.1	22750131.95
3	**0.998650102**	**0.001349898**	**1349.9**	**1349898.032**
4	0.999968329	3.16712E-05	31.7	31671.24184
4.5	**0.999996602**	**3.39767E-06**	**3.4**	**3397.673134**
5	0.999999713	2.86652E-07	0.3	286.6516541
6	**0.999999999**	**9.86588E-10**	**0.0**	**0.9865877**
7	1	1.27987E-12	0.0	0.001279865
7.5	**1**	**3.18634E-14**	**0.0**	**3.18634E-05**

targets are not easily achievable and may not be affordable. The goal of Six Sigma is already too demanding and expensive for many organizations to benefit from it.

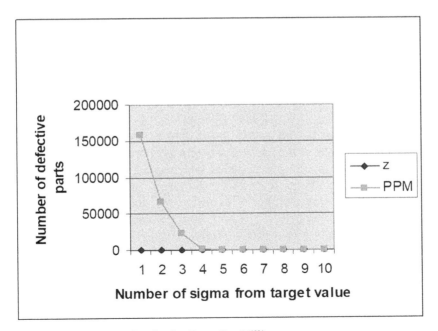

Figure 9.2. Number of Defective Parts Per Million.

TRAINING FOR SIX SIGMA

There are different levels of attainment in the training for Six Sigma. We shall discuss the popular ones notably, champion, black belt, green belt, and master black belt. Each level contains specific body of knowledge and shows level of sophistication in both knowledge and implementation of Six Sigma. However, as Hoerl (2001) has noted, due to the lack of standardization in the certification process for these belts, a wide range of variation may be observed. So, in fact, these certification programs are not indeed practicing Six Sigma. All black belts are not the same neither are all green belts. For our interested reader, we should briefly and in general describe these identified levels of training.

- Champion—A champion is a business leader or senior executive who has the responsibility to allocate resources for training and projects. A champion participates in project reviews and serves as a mentor to Black belts and a liaison to top management.
- Master black belt—This is the highest rank in hierarchy. Master black belts have a much higher level of sophistication both in the use of statistical tools and in management skills. They are teachers and leaders. They oversea projects done by black belts and green belts and channel those projects to achieve organizational mission. They participate in developing programs for the black belts.
- Black belt—Black belts are generally practitioners who understand advanced quality improvement tools such as design of experiments, statistical process control, reliability, robust design, and so forth. They are knowledgeable on the basic applications of these statistical tools. According to the information from American Society of Quality pasted on its website, "The Certified Six Sigma Black Belt is a professional who can explain Six Sigma philosophies and principles, including supporting systems and tools. The Black Belt should demonstrate team leadership, understand team dynamics, and assign team member roles and responsibilities. They have a thorough understanding of and can use all aspects of the DMAIC model in accordance with Six Sigma principles. They have basic knowledge of lean enterprise concepts, are able to identify non-value-added elements and activities and are able to use specific tools" (http://www.asq.org/cert/types/sixsigma/bok.html). They are also trained on QFD, FMEA (Failure Mode and Effects Analysis), and design techniques. They are technical leaders and change agents in the organization and use the tools of Six Sigma to achieve the maximum cost reduction for the organization.

- Green belt—They are key role is to ensure the success of a Six Sigma initiative. They are usually involved in selecting and defining projects, developing project objectives, information and data acquisition, and statistical analysis. They are also change managers and must be efficient in the application of Six Sigma tools and methodologies. So, the primary duties for green belts include gathering data and managing small projects. There work complements the black belt. They execute the principles and practices of Six Sigma on a day-to-day basis. They build on the efforts of Black Belts and may even lead their own improvement projects.

Six Sigma in Hospitals:

Virtua Health, a four hospital system servicing Southern New Jersey and Philadelphia is a nonprofit integrated delivery system. It implemented Six Sigma in September 2000 to improve patient satisfaction and financial performance. Virtua Health has undertaken projects in nearly every aspect of its business. A Six Sigma congestive heart failure (CHF) team found that outcomes, length of stay, and treatment pathways were highly variable. Six Sigma was used to define the causes of variation, allowing the team to develop solutions that involved patients and families in the delivery of care. The CHF team was also able to streamline the process, resulting in a significant decrease in length of stay from 6.2 to 4.6 days (Ettinger, 2001). Virtua Health's Six Sigma projects also included improving patient satisfaction, operating room throughput, nurse retention and reducing medication errors.

REFERENCES

Banuelas, R., & Antony, J. (2004). Six Sigma or design for Six Sigma? *The TQM Magazine, 16*(4), 250–263.

Basu, R. (2001). Six Sigma to FIT Sigma: The new wave of operational excellence. Retrieved from September 27, 2004, from https://nanopdf.com/download/six-sigma-to-fit-sigma-performance-excellence_pdf

Easton, G., and Jarrel, S., (1998), "The effects of Total Quality Management on corporate performance," *Journal of Business, 71*, 253–307.

Ettinger, W. (2001). Six sigma adapting GE's lesson to health care. *Trustee 54*(8), 10–16.

Goh, T. N., & Xie, M. (2004). Improving on the Six Sigma paradigm. *The TQM Magazine, 16*(4), 235–240.

Harry, M., & Shroeder, R. (2000). *Six Sigma: The breakthrough strategy revolutionizing the world's top corporations.* New York, NY: Doubleday.

Hoerl, R.W. (2001). Six Sigma black belts: What do they need to know? *Journal of Quality Technology, 33*(4), 391–406.

Kuei, C. H., & Madu, C. N. (2003). Customer-centric Six Sigma quality and reliability management. *International Journal of Quality and Reliability Management, 20*(8), 954–964.

Mitra, A. (2004). Six Sigma education: A critical role for academia. *The TQM Magazine, 16*(4), 293–302.

Nave, D. (2002). How to compare Six Sigma, lean and the theory of constraints. *Quality Progress, 35*(3), 73–79.

Sterman, J. D., Keating, E. K., Oliva, R., Repenning N. P., & Rockart, S. (1999). Overcoming the improvement paradox. *European Management Journal, 17,* 120–134.

CHAPTER 10

STAKEHOLDER VERSUS CUSTOMER IN PRODUCT DESIGN

In the previous chapters, we have focused our attention on identifying customer requirements and having such requirements satisfied through design. That focus tends to suggest a product-dependent analysis of customer requirements. Indeed, such is true. However, QFD's role can be expanded beyond that. Companies listen to the voice of the customer so they can compete and survive in business. QFD is just a tool that could help them achieve the goal of designing customer requirements into the product or service. In this chapter, we shall expand the definition of customer. Here, we define a customer as anyone or entity that is affected by the product or service offered by a firm. To avoid any confusion in the use of terminology, we shall refer to this class of customers as stakeholders. Thus, stakeholders are individuals or groups that are affected by the product or service offered by a firm. This definition of stakeholders will lead us to our new line of thoughts on how QFD's role in product design could further help the firm to be more competitive.

THE ROLE OF STAKEHOLDERS IN THE MARKET PLACE

It is important that firms understand who their customers are and what influence their purchase decisions. Obviously, the essence of any busi-

The House of Quality in a Minute:
A Guide to Quality Function Deployment (3rd Ed.), pp. 105–114
Copyright © 2020 by Information Age Publishing

ness is to satisfy the customer and by so doing, customer loyalty can be maintained. The customer will continue to patronize the business and that business will not only continue to survive but will thrive and do well financially. Successful businesses attract more investors and can generate new capital for reinvestment. Thus, businesses that have high customer loyalty tend to also grow faster. However, when a business fails to maintain customer loyalty, it will continue to report financial loses, become a riskier investment and shareholders lose confidence and pull out from the business. Thus, the survival of any business can be linked directly to the business's ability to retain customers.

However, since the 1980s, the market environment has gradually changed. In the past, a customer could assess the quality of a product or service by checking for certain attributes that relate directly to the performance of the product. Once such attributes maintain a high-quality standard, the customer's business is assured. This is no longer so. Customer's no longer look only at the intrinsic product quality attributes. In fact, many customers tend to assume that such attributes should be basic requirements for products. They however, look at other factors such as, the environmental content of the product or service (i.e., energy consumption, pollution, recyclability, etc.) and may in fact, look at the overall performance of the business in other areas such as social responsibility to the community (Madu, & Kuei, 1995). In other words, focusing on designing products or services that meet the intrinsic needs of the customer may not be enough to gain market shares, maintain customer loyalty and survive in today's business environment. Businesses need to adopt a more holistic view of their operations and guided by vision, will be able to identify the core factors that drive customers to support a business. Such core factors should be integrated in product design in order to satisfy the customer. This goal can be achieved if rather than trying to satisfy customer requirements through QFD, the firm aims to satisfy stakeholder requirements. It should be noted that stakeholder requirements also include the intrinsic needs of the customer that must be present in any product or service offered by the firm. However, it goes beyond that to include extraneous factors that may be part of the "unspoken" requirements of the customer. In this era of information age, customers are more enlightened and well educated. They are asking questions and easily getting answers.

The Internet , social media, and other mediums for communication have also helped in making information instantly available to customers. They are taking more proactive roles in their lives and are responding by taking actions to protect their interests. One area customers have shown increased focus is in the area of environmental protection and to ignore it will be to ignore the future. Furthermore, social responsibility and integrity issues are becoming prominent in assessing the performance of a firm.

Madu and Kuei (1995) introduced the concept of strategic total quality management and defined it as a quality measure of the overall performance of the firm. This performance assessment is not limited to the intrinsic values offered by a product or service but also on how the product or service affects the quality of life of people around it. The growing importance of social responsibility and environmental protection issues can also be seen from the increase in growth of social choices stocks. Evidently, business survives if it can satisfy customers by meeting customer requirements and customer requirements do not have to be limited to the direct value derived from the product. For example, a customer purchasing a toner cartridge for a laser printer may be interested in the quality of the print (i.e., clarity and brightness), duration of the cartridge (i.e., number of pages printed), and so forth, but may at the same time, be concerned with the emission of gases or chemical substances from the cartridge, disposal of expired cartridges. We shall elaborate more on this and why and how QFD teams should respond. A recent case in point is the call by privacy groups such as Junkbusters and Electronic Privacy Information Center to boycott Intel products over new technology by Intel that would identify consumers as they surf through the Internet. These groups argue that customer profiles will be collected and sold through this new technology. This action has attracted publicity as some lawmakers are calling on Intel to reconsider the introduction of this product (Bridis, 1999). The need to advocate stakeholder analysis in product design can also be supported by studies that show consumers are increasingly willing to pay more for environmentally friendly products [Natarajan, 1993; Vandermerwe, & Oliffe, 1990]. Also, the proliferation of new environmental laws most of which have come about as a result of public outrage over the degradation of the environment suggest a need for corporate rethinking of environmental policies (Madu, 1996). Many companies are indeed seeing environmental and corporate social responsibility programs as good for business today. Hence, we hear of companies introducing new environmental products like the introduction of electric cars and hybrid vehicles; the use of genetically engineered micro-organisms to absorb carbon dioxide; marketing of industrial equipment that absorb sulfur oxides and nitrous oxides from smoke stacks of steel and electric power plants; increased use of sewage-control and sludge-treatment equipment to avoid ocean dumping of wastes; low-emission incinerators for both liquid and solid wastes to combat the landfill problems (Madu, & Kuei 1995). Indeed, corporations are taking notice of these emerging customer requirements and are doing something. Several companies now have in-house programs to deal with environmental issues. For example, 3M maintains an environmental program known as the 3Ps—Pollution Prevention Pays; Chevron maintains a program known as SMART—Save Money And Reduce Toxic, and Dow Chemical maintains a program known as WRAP—Waste Reduction Always Pays. In addition, the increasing attention given by more than 100 countries to ISO 14000 series of environmental management systems shows that it is about time to consider other factors beyond the direct product quality.

Corporate alliance with interest groups is also on the rise. For example, the fast-food restaurant giant McDonald's had an alliance with the Environmental Defense Fund (EDF) to develop a way to reduce solid waste. The result is a switch from polystyrene shells to paper wrap. Pacific Gas and Electric Company often seeks the advice of Natural Resources Defense Council. New England Electric System worked with The Conservation Law Foundation to develop its 20-year strategic plan (Madu, 1996). This resulted in a focus on the use of renewable resources and recycling of wastes to generate electricity. These alliances are healthy for the businesses because they help increase the competitiveness of the firm. The corporation adopts a holistic perspective of its environment and works with those whose actions and reactions may affect the successful introduction of a product. When the QFD team is expanded to include not just members of the cross-functional units in a firm but stakeholders often referred to as active participants, the opposing views of both groups can be better understood by team members. It is possible that some of the concerns of the stakeholder team may not be effectively treated through design. In that case, other remedies may be sought when applicable. When these interest groups work amicably with the firm, their participation can help reduce some of the negative perceptions and confrontation that may publicly exist.

STAKEHOLDER ANALYSIS FOR QFD APPLICATION

Traditionally, the QFD team consists of members of the cross-functional units within the firm. The QFD team can be expanded to include important stakeholders. The steps to include them can be conducted as shown in Table 10.1.

Table 10.1.
Stakeholder Analysis

Step 1:	Identify the stakeholders and their courses of action.
Step 2:	Identify the major stakeholders that can affect the competitiveness of the firm and include them in the QFD team.
Step 3:	Identify stakeholders' requirements.
Step 4:	Develop a list of design requirements to satisfy stakeholder requirements.
Step 5:	Establish a dialog with the stakeholder teams

(Table continues on next page)

Table 10.1.
Stakeholder Analysis (Continued)

Step 6	Benchmark corporate performance on the stakeholders' requirements and technical targets against those of the firm's competitors.
Step 7:	Identify areas for improvement and work with stakeholders to develop a sustained plan.
Step 8:	Develop a long-term association with stakeholders.
Step 9:	Conduct periodic environmental scanning to determine when to add new stakeholders and when to remove inactive ones.

Step 1: Identify the Stakeholders and Their Courses of Action

It is important to know who your stakeholders are just as it is important to know who your customers are. A comprehensive list of these stakeholders will be a beginning point as well as their courses of action. For example, how influential are these stakeholder teams? Are they likely to influence the customer perception of the product and the firm? Remember that in marketing, you do not want any negative ads. Stakeholder teams that can reach a wider audience and that have a track record of being on the right sides of the issue cannot only influence potential customers but also legislators to enact new laws that may affect the performance of the firm. These stakeholder teams should be treated as active participants and integrated in the product planning and design stages. The list of stakeholders generated at this stage should not be static. In fact, the process of stakeholder list generation should be ongoing as new groups emerge over time and may actually have more direct impact on the firm's effectiveness.

Step 2: Identify the Major Stakeholders That Can Affect the Competitiveness of the Firm and Include Them in the QFD Team

Some of the issues in this step were discussed in Step 1. However, more importantly, the firm should not be consumed with including all stakeholders in its product planning and design. In fact, this may be counterproductive and may make the firm ineffectual. It is important to analyze each stakeholder generated in Step 1 and narrow the list to the significant few. There are many interest groups that are redundant and competing against each other just as in business. The focus should, however, be on working with those that have the capacity to influence potential customers. The point of view or perception of influential stakeholder teams should be considered in the product planning and design stages.

Step 3: Identify Stakeholders' Requirements

Once the right stakeholder teams are identified and brought into the QFD team, it is important to identify their product or service requirements. Obviously, this will focus on both the intrinsic and extrinsic values of the product or services. The requirements generated should also be evaluated to eliminate redundancies and should also be rank ordered. This will enable the firm to focus its limited resources on solving the critical requirements of the stakeholder teams. Stakeholders should also be allowed to suggest strategies to satisfy their product requirements and offer perspectives on their expectations of future outcomes.

Step 4: Develop a List of Design Requirements to Satisfy Stakeholder Requirements

The QFD team develops design requirements based on stakeholders' requirements. The design requirements should clearly outline how each of the stakeholders' requirements could be satisfied through design. Furthermore, potential tradeoffs should be identified as well as the inability to satisfy some of the stakeholders' requirements through design.

Step 5: Establish a Dialog With the Stakeholder Teams

The QFD team should hold a dialog with stakeholder teams so both sides can understand how design requirements can be used to satisfy customer requirements. This will also help to resolve issues on trade-offs, and infeasibility of some stakeholder requirements. In fact, this is a learning process where both sides of the aisle will understand each other perspective better, offer different scenarios to problem solving, and develop an acceptable strategy for both parties.

Step 6: Benchmark Corporate Performance on the Stakeholders' Requirements and Technical Targets Against Those of the Firm's Competitors

With a mutually acceptable design requirement to satisfy stakeholder requirements, the process of benchmarking can begin. The firm benchmarks itself against its major competitors. This stage is identical to that shown in Figure 4.4.

Step 7: Identify Areas for Improvement and Work With Stakeholders to Develop a Sustained Plan

Through benchmarking, the firm can position itself, assess its strengths, weaknesses, opportunities, and threats. Furthermore, it can develop capabilities where it lacks one in order to compete effectively.

Step 8: Develop a Long-Term Association With Stakeholders

Long-term association with stakeholders is important. It helps the firm to obtain timely information about its environment. More importantly, by stakeholder teams participating in making critical product planning and design, they are more likely to accept responsibility for the final product. This may transcend to maintaining customer loyalty, increasing competitiveness, and assuring the survival of the firm. It is very important that the firm seeks to work with its active participants. These participants influence the survival of the firm. The focus of the firm should be to design and produce the product or service as its stakeholder groups which include consumer groups view as important to them and not as the designers view to be important.

Step 9: Conduct Periodic Environmental Scanning to Determine When to Add New Stakeholders and When to Remove Inactive Ones

The business environment is changing quickly. We are often over-burdened by information overload and as more information is made available, various people have different reactions to the information. In return, new groups are being formed and hence, new stakeholders are emerging. Also, stakeholder groups that have achieved their goals or are unable to follow with the dynamism of the environment often disappear. The firm should periodically, evaluate these stakeholder groups as to their performance in their communities. Inactive groups should be dropped from the list and new active ones should be added. Once the firm remains in business, it must continue to deal with groups whose actions affect its survival.

STRATEGIZING QFD

Our discussion on the use of stakeholders in building the QFD is strategic. We can sum this discussion up with two charts Figure 10.1 and Figure 10.2. First, we shall discuss Figure 10.1.

Figure 10.1.   Stakeholder analysis.

This figure starts with information gathering. This is the process of generating information on the stakeholders, getting to know them, and integrating them in the QFD decision-making process. The stakeholders develop a list of their requirements and work with the QFD team to match design requirements against stakeholder requirements. This takes both strategic and tactical roles. With the strategic, the firm adopts a more holistic view of its operation, links its competitiveness and survivability to the acceptance of its products or services by its stakeholders. As a result, it looks on the stakeholders to understand the key to competitiveness and survivability. The tactical phase, however, deals with the actual design planning and production. This is the responsibility of the QFD team. However, the QFD team knows that there are tradeoffs that may be involved in trying to satisfy stakeholders' requirements and that certain requirements may not be feasible. It engages in a dialogue with the stakeholder teams on these potential tactical problems and aims to arrive at an amicable solution to this problem. Partnership is a key component of Figure 10.1 as it shows that rather than an adversarial relationship that often exists between businesses and interest groups, that indeed they could develop a partnership to achieve their common goals. Such partnership is good for business since it helps the two opposing views to come together, understand their different worldviews, become more pragmatic, and resolve potential conflicts productively. When these teams interact and share information, they can understand the different perspectives that may shape ones decision making.

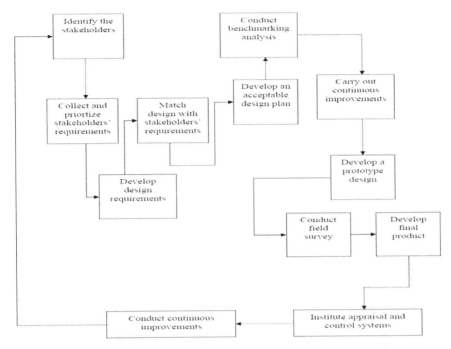

Figure 10.2.   Strategic product planning.

Figure 10.2 is an articulation of the steps outlined in Table 10.1 with the exception of the last section that starts with "Develop a prototype design." Indeed, that is the DO stage of the design process. We discussed this in Chapter 7 with Figure 7.4. Basically, this figure again shows that the incorporation of stakeholders in the QFD team will still make the process pragmatic but offer the added advantage that the "customer" or "stakeholder" is directly involved in every stage of the product design and production.

CONCLUSION

In this chapter, we focused on the use of stakeholders rather than the customer in generating customer requirement for the QFD chart. Stakeholder is a broader definition of customer to include all those whose actions or reactions may affect the competitiveness of the firm. We term these "active participants." Furthermore, the role of stakeholder team is expanded. Rather than just finding out what their requirements are, they should be part of the QFD team in designing and planning for the product. It is important that the stakeholder team understands the need for tradeoffs, the limitations of the firm, and the technical infeasibility of some requirements that may emerge. Furthermore, the use of stakeholder teams can help the firm to get acceptance of its product by customers who are represented by the stakeholders. If stakeholders participate in the critical phases of decision making regarding the product, they are more likely to accept the final outcome. We have also noted that purchasing decisions today are not entirely dependent on product quality but also on the other extrinsic factors that are part of the package that goes along with the product. Customers these days look at the environmental content of the product and evaluate the social responsibility of the firm to its community. These extrinsic factors are values that customers often share and these may influence their purchase decisions. Therefore, a QFD chart that captures all customer requirements intrinsic in a product but fails to look at these extrinsic factors will still not be successful. Corporations today take expanded role. They must be seen as caring and responsive to the needs of the society. It is imperative that they identify what the society expects from them. On that note, it is important that influential stakeholders that represent segments of the society be part of this decision-making process.

SELF STUDY QUESTIONS

1. What are the steps needed to include stakeholders in QFD application?
2. Why do we need stakeholders?
3. Are stakeholders the same as stockholders? What are the differences?

REFERENCES

Bridis, T. (1999, January 25). Privacy groups to boycott Intel over new chip. *Associated Press.*
Madu, C. N., & Kuei, C.-H. (1995). *Strategic Total Quality Management: Corporate performance and product quality.* Westport, CT: Quorum Books.
Madu, C. N. (1996). *Managing green technologies for global competitiveness.* Westport, CT: Quorum Books.
Natarajan, R. (1993). Implementing TEQ: Steal shamelessly from TQM. In *Proceedings of Decision Sciences Institute* (pp. 1870–1872). Washington, DC.
Vandermerwe, S., & Oliffe, M. D. (1990). Consumers Drive Corporations Green. *Long Range Planning, 23*(6), 10–16.

CHAPTER 11

QFD AND CONCURRENT ENGINEERING

We are witnessing the rapid proliferation of new products. Product life cycles are getting shorter. Rapid response to the market is key to competing effectively in today's market. Manufacturers are taking notice and are reacting accordingly by cutting down the time it takes to introduce new products into the market. Concurrent engineering has emerged as an approach to achieve this rapid market response. Concurrent engineering is basically, the use of a multidisciplinary team to provide the design and development of products and processes simultaneously and rapidly. This is in response to the changing marketing environment where time management is key to improving the bottom line. Concurrent engineering takes a holistic view of the product. Rather than each department operating independently and treating its tasks in product development as independent, the different functional units within the firm work as a team and sees their tasks as interdependent. Concurrent engineering is a business strategy where product development is done in parallel at every stage of the product development process. The focus is to make optimal use of the firm's resources. It is a shift from the traditional manufacturing processes that is vertical in nature to a horizontal process that is lateral and flat. We shall use Figure 11.1 to illustrate.

The House of Quality in a Minute:
A Guide to Quality Function Deployment (3rd Ed.), pp. 115–123

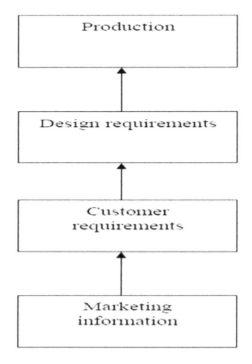

Figure 11.1. Traditional Manufacturing Process.

VERTICAL VERSUS HORIZONTAL PRODUCT REALIZATION

With the vertical product realization process, the triggering point for new product development or redesigning of existing product is marketing information. The marketing department interfaces with customers or end users, obtains marketing information on customer needs and desires and relays the information to manufacturing. The need for a product is borne out of this information and the product if developed must satisfy this existing need. Marketing may further organize marketing research to develop specifications for the new product, as they believe the customer may prefer. For example, what features should be in the product that will attract customer attention? Let us take for example a desktop computer. The capacity of the hard drive, the RAM, or even the inclusion of features such as webcam may be desirable features that the customer is looking for. This is really a process of generating customer requirements as we showed in the construction of the QFD chart. Once this is done, the next stage is to develop design requirements. The design requirements look at how customer requirements can be achieved through design. For example, what size of hard drive should be provided? What is the most ergonomic way to design the computer hardware? What design of keyboard will be more appropriate to satisfying customer requirement? In the QFD chart we also went through the benchmarking process. However, once an acceptable design is developed, the next phase is production. Through the production process, a new product is developed that may satisfy the customer need. This vertical product realization process is, however, very limited in some aspects. Some of the limitations are:

1. The functional departments are independent. Each department does its job and moves the next task down a sequential line. For example, the role of marketing is different from designing and designing is different from manufacturing in product conceptualization and development. Even though these departments work for the overall goals of the organization, they are not unified as one body and each unit may suboptimize and may not really understand each other's perspectives and worldviews.

2. Duplication of tasks and waste are encouraged. For example, design by not understanding the production system well enough may design products that may not be easily produced. Furthermore, there is backtracking of information. The product designed may not really satisfy some of the customer requirements and marketing may come back to design with a problem.

3. Quality is compromised. When there is a lack of quality in any stage of the process, the product is sent back to that phase for fixture. This creates wastes both in time of product design and production and in terms of the resources that are dedicated to the product.

4. The lead-time to introduce new product or redesigned product into the market is longer as a result of the back and forth movement between the departments, quality problems, and so forth. The effect of this is that with the shorter product life cycles, the firm may not be competitive in today's fast-paced marketing environment. Furthermore, production cycle time is longer as we move through this vertical chain of the product design and development.

5. Due to the long production cycle time, lower quality, lower efficiency of the independent departments, and slower market introduction, higher costs are incurred. Customers also expect to pay higher for the product. The firm's slow entrance into the marketplace implies loss of market share and lack of competitiveness.

6. Customer satisfaction is low as products may not be designed and produced right the first time around. The firm spends more time

trying to rectify the problem rather than trying to continuously improve the quality of the product. Efficiency and the performance of the entire firm are affected, and manufacturing and production costs go up. The company's market share gradually erodes as it lacks competitiveness in today's dynamically changing market.

With the problems outlined above, it is better to adopt a horizontal product realization process. This is, indeed, what we achieve through concurrent engineering. Figure 11.2 is used as an illustration.

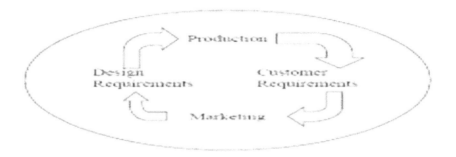

Figure 11.2.   Concurrent Engineering

HORIZONTAL PRODUCT REALIZATION PROCESS

Notice that Figure 11.2 shows a flat structure for the product realization process. Each major component of product design and development as shown in Figure 11.1 is contained here. However, there is no hierarchical structure on information flow. All the functional units work in parallel, collect and analyze information the same time and make timely decisions on product design and development. The key here is that information flow is facilitated and there is ongoing interaction between members of the cross-functional units that work as a team in the product design and development. When marketing offers information on customer requirements for example, the design unit can immediately discuss the feasibility of such requirements and how they may be designed into the product. Manufacturing can evaluate the design and identify production problems or effective production strategies; finance and accounting can discuss the viability of the project and the costing. All the parties understand exactly what must be done; where to scale down; and how to improve the product design and development. More importantly, they come to understand each other and how their respective functions are inter-related and aim to achieve organizational goals. It is through such cooperation that the organization's goals and objectives are articulated. Members of the team can then work harmoniously to satisfy customer needs. The benefits of concurrent engineering are numerous. Through concurrent engineering, all the problems listed under vertical product realization process can be alleviated. In addition, the following benefits accrue:

1. Product design and development times are significantly reduced. As a result, new products can be offered to the market on a timely basis. There will be rapid response to market needs. Furthermore, existing products can be easily redesigned, upgraded, and modified in a lesser time and at lower costs to satisfy customer needs.
2. Quality is very high as products are produced right the first time. The communication and interaction between the functional units who work in parallel as concurrent engineering team members, help to ensure that problems observed at each stage of the product development can be easily resolved.
3. The key to concurrent engineering is to improve quality, reduce production cost, and reduce the delivery time of product to the market. When these goals are achieved, efficiency and performance are significantly improved. There is no backtracking as we mentioned with the vertical product realization process.
4. The firm is competitive as it responds faster to market changes. Its resources are optimized as the firm aims to satisfy its customers timely and maintain their loyalty. Thus, market shares are maintained, and new markets may be gained. Customer satisfaction is high.
5. Time is effectively managed. The time to carry out tasks are cut down since redundancies and backtracking are eliminated.

QFD AND CONCURRENT ENGINEERING

As we have seen, concurrent engineering is actually a business strategy. It requires an overhaul of existing organizational structure to allow the functional units within the firm to operate in a team form. The concurrent engineering (CE) team or the CE team as they are often referred to, works through the product design and development stages to ensure timely response to the dynamic market environment. The aim is to drive down costs and product development time by making optimal use of the firm's resources. Although the term concurrent engineering sounds very technical, it relies on other tools to achieve its goals. QFD is one such tool that is frequently used by CE teams. Remarkably, the goals of QFD and concurrent engineering are similar. QFD for example, uses cross-functional teams in product development stage. This is also done with concurrent engineering. However, QFD as we have shown in previous chapters, can help the CE team to actually priortize customer requirements and develop a fit between customer requirements and design requirements. Furthermore, the issue of tradeoffs and benchmarking can be better understood through the application of QFD in a concurrent engineering environment. This process, however, should not be limited to the product design. In fact, concurrent engineering takes a "cradle-to-grave" approach with respect to the product. The CE team follows the product development process from the product conception to the development stage, to the end of the product's life. It is a strategy that follows the product through its life cycle.

CE team is also not limited to the internal units within the firm. In fact, the stakeholder approach we discussed in Chapter 10 is applicable here. CE team will be more effective if the team comprises of internal units as well as other stakeholders. Since the goal is to design and produce products on timely basis, it is important that stakeholders contribute to this decision-making process. As we mentioned in Chapter 9, stakeholders are those who may actively influence or be influenced by the product. Therefore, the CE team should include consumer interest groups, suppliers and vendors, as well as the members of the functional units within the firm. Once the CE team is formed, QFD becomes a useful tool to help them arrive at decisions. However, it is important to understand other issues that may affect the success of concurrent engineering and the application of QFD to solve product design and development problems.

SUCCESSFUL APPLICATION OF
CONCURRENT ENGINEERING

Concurrent engineering is a new management philosophy that inter-plays with a firm's business strategy. As a result, it is not easily implemented without a hitch. The success of concurrent engineering applications depends on a new attitude within the firm. It is a strategic weapon that can drive the firm to success and make it competitive but, in order to achieve all these, some hurdles must be overcome.

1. Management commitment and support—As Figure 11.2 shows, concurrent engineering advocates a flat organization. This is contrary to the hierarchical nature of both authority and information flow that exist in traditional organizations. Functional departments

must be made to understand that the joint efforts of all departments are needed to make the firm more efficient and competitive. Top management developing clear missions and vision for the organization could achieve this goal. The different departments must understand their role in helping the firm achieve its goals. It should also be clear that there is no internal competition between the departments and that their activities are inter-related and synergistic. Management must support the efforts of the CE team and provide the necessary resources needed to make them effective.

2. Management involvement is required. It is not enough to support the CE team. Management should view CE team as a strategic unit and the leader of the team should be a senior executive of the firm. Yet, the CE team should be empowered to make decisions otherwise, the fast response rate expected from concurrent engineering will not be achieved.

3. CE team members should be trained appropriately on the roles of teams, problem solving, and conflict resolution. Communication and sharing of information are one of the ways that conflict could be resolved. Members need to understand the different perspectives under which they operate and should be open minded. Conflicts must surely arise within such a group formation. However, conflicts are not necessarily bad and can be made productive.

4. The corporate climate should be supportive of teamwork. The CE team should not be the only arm of the firm where teamwork is encouraged. In fact, the atmosphere must change to reflect a new business strategy and a new management philosophy with the goal of transforming the organization.

5. Management practices advocated in the 1980s that contributed to the failures of Western management styles should be examined and avoided. Deming (1985) discussed these problems extensively and clearly outlined them in his 14 points. It is important that the organization takes this path if it intends to achieve success with concurrent engineering.

Concurrent Engineering: Successful implementation

Product development process at Champion Road Machinery Ltd. has evolved into the use of concurrent engineering. This required a transformation of the organization to change its processes by changing the way people think in the organization. According to David Ross, vice president of engineering says "We had to totally reengineer our development process, and adopt not only a new process, but a whole new attitude." Concurrent engineering is an evolving process that can be adapted to company requirements. Champion is benefiting from this process and claims to have sharply increased sales and profits (Thorpe, 1995).

Concurrent Engineering

General Electric's Aircraft Engines Division used concurrent engineering to develop the engine for the new F/A-18E/F. The concurrent engineering teams achieved 20% to 60% reductions in design and procurement cycle times during the full-scale component tests, which preceded full engine testing. Problems surfaced earlier and were dealt with more efficiently than they would have been with the traditional development process. Cycle times in the design and fabrication of some components dropped from an estimated 22 weeks to 3 weeks (Start, n.d.).

CONCLUSION

In this chapter, we discussed concurrent engineering and QFD. We noted that both aim to achieve the same goal. However, concurrent engineering is a business strategy that is based on a cross-functional team that could include stakeholders. The CE team works in parallel through product design, development, and disposition. The CE team is empowered to make timely product decisions to respond swiftly to the competitive environment. Concurrent engineering is the wave to the future in a dynamic competitive environment and operates effectively in a TQM-based organizational culture. QFD on the other hand, is a tool that could enable the CE team to understand customer requirements, design requirements to meet customer needs into the product, and develop competitive strategies to assure successful introduction into the market. The goal here is to ensure that products of high quality are introduced timely into the market.

SELF STUDY QUESTIONS

1. What is concurrent engineering?
2. What is the trigger point for new product development with a vertical product realization process?
3. Mention some limitations of vertical product realization process.
4. Under the concurrent engineering process all the units work in
    _____.
5. Mention some benefits of concurrent engineering.
6. Discuss how QFD can work hand-in-hand with concurrent engineering.
7. Mention the hurdles to overcome successful application of concurrent engineering in a firm.

REFERENCES

Thorpe, P. A. (1995, October). Concurrent engineering: The key to success in today's competitive environment. *IIE Solutions. Norcross, 27*(10), 10.

Start, J. (n.d.). A few words about concurrent engineering. Retrieved from http://www.johnstark.com/fwcc.html

Deming, W. E. (1985). Transformation of Western style of management. *Interfaces, 15*(3), 6–11.

Deming, W. E. (1986). *Out of the crisis*. Cambridge, MA: MIT Press.

Deming, W. E. (1993). *The new economics for industry, government, education*, Cambridge, MA: MIT Press.

CHAPTER 12

QFD, COST CONTROL, AND PRODUCTIVITY IMPROVEMENT

Quality programs are supported only if they can help to improve the bottom-line. In all the preceding chapters, we have focused on the role of QFD in making the firm more competitive. This we stated will come about if customer satisfaction is achieved. Customers become loyal to the firm if they are satisfied. They patronize the business and spread good words about the products and services they are receiving from the firm. The business in return, will be able to increase its market share, invest in new technologies and research and development, and will be able to offer improved products and services over time. In a nutshell, the firm becomes more competitive. Yet, high quality does not necessarily mean that profits will be high. It is important to ensure that the cost of achieving high quality is kept under control. A typical example is Wallace Company, which won the coveted Malcolm Baldrige National Quality Award in 1991 but went bankrupt thereafter. Analysts have blamed the financial problems of Wallace Company on not keeping tabs on its quality costs. It is therefore imperative that any discussion about the role of quality in any business should also investigate cost control and productivity improvement issues. In this chapter, we shall tie in QFD, cost control, and productivity improvement.

The House of Quality in a Minute:
A Guide to Quality Function Deployment (3rd Ed.), pp. 125–133
Copyright © 2020 by Information Age Publishing

125

We shall also, borrow from the works of eminent leaders in the field of total quality management notably, Joseph M Juran and Edward W Deming.

COST CONTROL

Every successful business must have a proper control of its costs. It is generally accepted that the average cost of poor quality is in the range of 15 to 20% of total sales [Chase & Aquilano, 1995). However, as we embark on company-wide quality management, it is difficult to keep track of the sources of these quality costs. And, if the sources of the cost of poor quality can not be isolated, it becomes difficult to control them. The lack of specificity on the sources of the cost of poor quality can distort the entire picture and lead to solving the wrong problems. Poor quality does have a significant impact on the success of the firm. It leads to increased waste of materials and resources. For example, increased number of scraps and rejects may be created, labor-hours may be used up in repeating tasks that should have been done right the first time, warranty costs and liability costs will go up, productivity will drop, and most importantly, customer dissatisfaction will be high. The effects of all these on the bottom-line are significant. For example, when customers are dissatisfied, they spread the news by word-of-mouth and raise alarm about the product or the firm. This may dissuade potential customers from purchasing the product and service. When this happens, the firm loses market share and lacks competitiveness. This impacts on the ability of the firm to continue providing products and services to its customers at a higher quality. A study by The Ernst & Young Quality Improvement Consulting Group (1988) states the following

> A potentially … devastating consequence of the bottom line is the reaction of the customer who receives a defective or otherwise unsatisfactory product or service. A recent survey showed that, while a satisfied customer will tell a few people about his or her experience, a dissatisfied person will tell an average of 19 others."

Obviously, the word-of-mouth is a devastating tool that the customer can use to discredit a firm's product or service when he or she is dissatisfied. This study further notes that dissatisfied customers rarely complain to the provider of poor quality goods and services. Also, when they complain through the marketing or service channels, their complaints rarely get the attention they deserve. The alternative has been to switch to a competing product or service.

Many of the problems with poor quality relate to poor product or service designs and product defects. Many of these problems could have been corrected before the product gets to the customer. QFD as a tool can help ensure that product design satisfies customer requirements. As shown in Chapter 11, the use of QFD and concurrent engineering can also help to eliminate defects in the product or service.

COST OF QUALITY (COQ)

Juran introduced the cost of quality (Juran & Gryna, 1988). He argues that in order to get top management to pay attention to quality, they must know the bottom-line or how poor quality affects the profit margin. Cost of quality relates to the costs to production as a result of defects or imperfection in the product. As we mentioned above, this cost could range from 15 to 20% of the sales revenue (Chase & Aquilano, 1995). Crsoby (1979) recommend that this cost should be under 2.5%. The premise behind controlling the cost of quality can be outlined as follows:

1. Prevention is cheaper than taking corrective actions. Thus, it is important to design and produce the product right the first time rather than aiming to correct defects when they do occur.
2. Performance is measurable. It is possible to measure the performance of the product or service against a metric or target specifications. The performance measures must meet or surpass the expectations of the customer.
3. Failures may result if poor quality items are designed and produced. The sources of failures can be studied, analyzed, and prevented.

There are four types of cost of quality. These are discussed below.

TYPES OF COST OF QUALITY

1. Appraisal costs—these include the costs of inspection, testing, and related activities that will ensure that the final product is free of defects. Here, we see how concurrent engineering and QFD can help to eliminate appraisal costs. As noted in Chapter 11, members of the CE team work in parallel with stakeholders to ensure that the final product meets customer expectations. Defects can be eliminated through a cradle-to-grave approach of the product. For example, designers can identify design problems that could be eliminated to satisfy customer requirements. However, manufacturing may detect imperfections in the process that may contribute to defects. Material selection may also be a source of defects in the product. These

sources of defects could be controlled before they occur. Inspection and testing of the product for defects could be limited if design and manufacturing strategies are supported through QFD and concurrent engineering, and care is taken in designing and producing the product or service.

2. Prevention costs—this cost is incurred in an attempt to prevent defects. Such costs include the cost of developing a work environment that supports the quality efforts of the organization, cost of design or redesign of the product or process, training costs, cost of the cradle-to-grave approach in manufacturing, cost of working with vendors and suppliers, cost of integrating QFD or CE teams with stakeholder teams. Prevention cost has the effect of pushing the proportion of defects down. Notice that prevention strategy involves more proactive role to control defects and manage quality. The use of QFD and CE are preventive in nature. They support the goal of producing high quality goods and services by focusing not only on design but on all phases of production that may affect the quality of the product. For example, by working with suppliers, the manufacturer can establish a quality guideline for incoming raw materials that will be in line with the quality imperatives of the firm. When we discussed quality control in Chapter 8, we noted that there are two causes of variation in a process: natural and special causes. We also noted that the operator has no control over natural causes of variation. An example of this is the selection of suppliers for raw materials. The top management makes this decision. Therefore, if the QFD team designs the right product and the supplier sends in poor quality materials to production, the firm will still not be able to satisfy customer requirements. The problem becomes systemic and only the top management can resolve it. This also highlights the importance of using concurrent engineering with QFD. It is seen here that in order to reduce the cost of poor quality, all parties that affect the product production process must participate at an early stage in developing the product. The CE team offers the opportunity of being inclusive of all significant players in the product development and production phases.

3. Internal Failure Costs—These costs deal with defects that are detected within the production system. Such include the costs of scraps, rejects and reworks before the product is shipped to the customer. These costs can be controlled if the product development stages through design and production are well guided.

4. External Failure Costs—These costs occur after the customer has received the product. External failure costs could be devastating to a firm. Some of the costs include warranty costs, liability costs, recall

costs, loss of customer goodwill, loss of customer loyalty, complaint costs, and societal costs.

All these four types of costs can be improved on by designing quality into the product and ensuring that only products of high quality are shipped to the customer. When the customer notices defect in the product or service, it is not easily resolved by replacing the product or maintaining the warranty agreement. As we cited above, many of the complaints may not be fed back to the manufacturer but those that matter most to the firm—customers—will come to know about the problems.

VIEWS ON COST OF QUALITY

The traditional view of cost of quality is that as prevention costs increase, the percentage of defect in the product will decrease. Conversely, failure costs are directly associated with the proportion of defects. As a result, there is an optimal proportion of defects where total quality cost is minimized. This is the problem with this traditional view. It suggests that after a point, prevention is ineffective and may in fact, be costly. This may challenge the concept of continuous improvement. There are several debates about this controversial view. As expected, leading quality experts also disagree on this issue. Proponents of cost of quality are quality leaders like Juran and Gryna (1988) Crosby (1979) while Deming believed that it is useless.

The modern view of cost of quality is that zero defects could be achieved. This view supports a focus on prevention and argues that prevention costs are fixed while failure costs keep rising. Figures 12.1 and 12.2 show these relationships.

External and internal failure costs are estimated to account for about 60 to 90% of total quality costs. Traditionally, the attempt has been to increase inspection in order to reduce external failure costs. However, this could be counterproductive as it pushes up the costs of appraisal and internal failure while external failure costs may decline. It is apparent that the cost of non-conformance associated with rework, rejects, and scraps will decline as quality is continuously improved and prevention is focused on. This suggests that QFD and CE have significant role in reducing the cost of quality especially since prevention cost is a constant. By designing and producing products and services to meet customer requirements, defects can be effectively prevented if QFD and CE are concurrently used. Through CE and QFD, the number of defective items made will be minimized thus keeping internal failure costs low; and there will be less appraisal as the products are made right the first time. Management must, therefore, make the necessary commitment to support QFD and CE teams so that

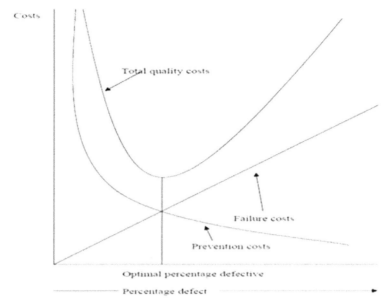

Figure 12.1.   Traditional Cost of Quality.

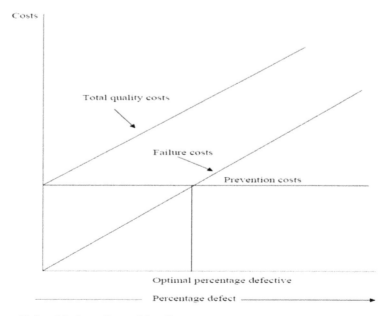

Figure 12.2.   Modern Cost of Quality.

high quality products that meet customer requirements can be designed, developed and produced.

QUALITY AND PRODUCTIVITY IMPROVEMENT

Deming (1986) demonstrated a link between quality and productivity improvement. This link is often referred to as Deming's chain reaction model. We have modified the Deming chain reaction model as shown in Figure 12.3.

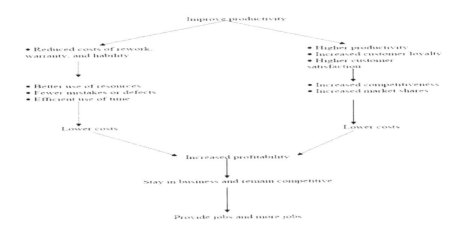

Figure 12.3. Link Between Quality and Productivity.

As shown in Figure 12.3, we can improve the quality of the product or service through the application of QFD. Quality improvement plays a significant role in the survival of a firm. For example, improvement in quality will lead to a reduction in the costs of quality we outlined above. It also, leads to higher productivity as less waste are incurred; increased customer loyalty is achieved, as customer satisfaction is higher. When the quality of the product or service is high, limited resources in terms of labor, material, and time are efficiently utilized. This will help the firm become more competitive and gain market shares. The large market share will help the firm benefit from economies of scale and this will help to drive costs down. When the product is perceived to offer higher value, it may also be possible to market the product at higher prices. When this is achieved, revenue is increased as well as profits. With increased profits, the firm is able to attract investors. New capital can flow into the business that will help it to modernize its facilities, innovate on new products and services, and invest on research and development. The firm will continue to grow, stay in business and remain competitive. As the company grows, it also offers an important social responsibility function to its community—that of providing jobs and more jobs.

Clearly, profitability, quality and the survival of the firm go hand in hand. A firm that lacks quality products and services cannot survive in today's competitive environment. Each firm must be able to define the value that its products or services offer to customers and aim to achieve quality at the highest level. QFD is emphatically, a tool that can help achieve that goal and when used concurrently with concurrent engineering, the firm is able to realize its dream of market growth.

Toyota Case

Toyota achieved remarkable success with QFD. It began to apply QFD to auto body for small vans in 1977. Two years later, Toyota reported a reduction in start-up costs of 20% and by 1984 the reduction was 61%, while the product development cycle was reduced by one third (McElroy, 1987). Toyota's supplier Aisin Warner, which supplies 98% of the transmissions, reduced the number of engineering changes during the product development, development time and start up cycle by half (Biren, 1998; Sullivan, 1986).

CONCLUSION

In this chapter, we have discussed the cost of quality and the link between quality and productivity. We have noted that offering customers products or services that satisfy their requirements may help to control most of the quality costs. Therefore, the QFD as a tool plays a significant role in achieving that goal. However, we have noted that concurrent engineering will be effective in conjunction with QFD since some of the problems of poor quality may not deal directly with poor designs. In fact, it is important that significant stakeholders in the CE team can help to evaluate any product design and development process and provide any necessary preventive strategies before the design and development of the product. By doing this, the cost of poor quality can be minimized. We also, contrasted the traditional and modern views of cost of quality and showed that unlike the traditional view, the prevention cost is fixed and the target is to achieve zero defects.

We ended the chapter by looking at the link between quality and productivity. We extended Deming's chain reaction model to show that in fact, improvement in quality may lead to reduction in cost of quality, higher productivity, lower costs, increased profitability, survivability and competitiveness of the firm. When the firm is competitive, it is able to expand and provide more jobs. QFD again is behind this link. It lets the manufacturer better understand its customers and to better offer products and services that will satisfy their needs. It is through QFD that quality and value can be defined into the product and services. Customer requirements can also be introduced into the product at a higher performance level but yet at lower costs if concurrent engineering team participates to develop the QFD.

SELF STUDY QUESTIONS

1. Outline the premises behind controlling the costs of quality.
2. List the types of costs of quality.
3. Which of the costs is the most important? Briefly discuss Deming's chain reaction model.

REFERENCES

Biren, P. (1998). Toyota: Review of QFD and related deployment techniques. *Journal of Manufacturing System.* Retrieved from http://www.findarticles.com/p/articles/mi_qa3685/is_199801/ai_n8765952s,

Chase, R. B., & Aquilano, N. J. (1995). Production and operations management—Manufacturing and services (7th ed.). Chicago, IL: Irwin.

Crosby, P. (1979). *Quality is free.* New York, NY: New American Library.

Deming, W. E. (1986). *Out of the crisis.* Cambridge, MA: MIT Center for Advanced Engineering Studies.

Ernst & Young Quality Improvement Consulting Group. (1988). *Total quality: An executive's guide for the 1990s,* Burr Ridge, IL: Irwin Professional Publishing.

Juran, J. M., & Gryna, F. M. (1988). *Juran's quality control handbook.* New York, NY: McGraw-Hill.

McElroy, J.(1987, June). "For whom are we building cars?" *Automotive Industries,* 68–70.

Sullivan, L. P. (1986). Quality function deployment. *Quality Progress, 19,* 39–50.

CHAPTER 13

QFD AND PROCESS CHANGE MANAGEMENT

For quality function deployment to be effective, it is imperative that processes are able to provide the needed products and services to perfection. Process management requires a review of the steps to create value in products and services. These processes must be capable to support the products or services that are being provided. Processes may change over time to respond to the dynamic needs of the customer and/or to respond to competition. QFD requires matching customer needs to design requirements. The aspect of design requirements involves the steps or processes to satisfy customer needs. It is imperative that these processes are effective and efficient. In other words, a highly capable process is needed to satisfy customer needs. Such processes should be robust and resilient and be able to continue to meet the changing needs of the customer.

In this chapter, we discuss how process efficiency and effectiveness can be achieved to continue to satisfy the needs of the customer.

The Process of Transition

John Fisher (2012) eloquently presented a personal transition curve that clearly shows the process of transition. Process change is key to achieving

The House of Quality in a Minute:
A Guide to Quality Function Deployment (3rd Ed.), pp. 135–143
Copyright © 2020 by Information Age Publishing
All rights of reproduction in any form reserved.

efficiency and effectiveness in today's highly competitive market. As shown in the personal transition curve presented as Figure 13.1, people are of major concern when we want to change the process. The process is basically how services and products are provided. This may involve the change of how tasks are being performed or change of technology to perform the tasks. However, the task or the technology must work with the people that are involved. It is not always easy to marry people to processes. As shown in the transition curve below, anxiety sets in when new processes are introduced. How do I cope with the new process? Will I be able to make it? Will I be retained in the system? These questions introduce some level of anxiety which also induces fear that may make one to wonder his position in the transition of the process. Personal survival is always a major issue when processes are introduced because new processes can impact change and change is not easily assimilated. However, people are different and there are those that crave for change and such will think it is about time to change the process. So while some may grapple with fear, others may bask in happiness because they believe the current process must be changed. Change does not come easy. There are those who will fall of the cliff in the process of change and there are those who may find it difficult to adapt and yet there are those who will adapt and run with the change process. Change is inevitable in today's dynamic and competitive environment. People must be carried along in the change process. When people adapt

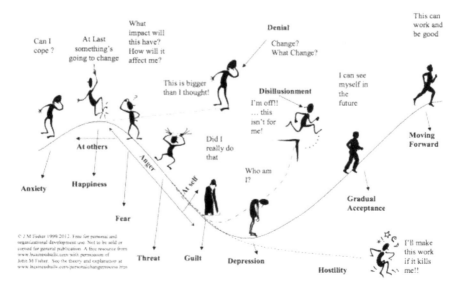

Figure 13.1. The Process of Transition.

and cope with change, they can work effectively with new technologies and new processes and will become smart workers. They will be more efficient and more effective.

To meet customer needs through design strategies, we need to know how best to satisfy the customer. This will involve a well laid out sequence of providing the services or producing the product. Each stage should be evaluated to ensure that value is added in providing the services. Those activities that are nonvalue adding should be deleted to streamline the process. What is then a process? A process involves a collection of interrelated tasks to solve a specific problem. It is therefore important that every process is mapped out to show the sequence and inter-relatedness of the different activities that are involved in performing a task. This is done by using a flow chart to depict the entire process. The use of flow chart helps to better understand how services are provided or how products are created. Each step of the process is evaluated by looking at the value that is created, the contributions of the step in creating value, identifying potential bottlenecks, and identifying redundant activities. Such activities that create bottlenecks or are redundant are removed to streamline the process. The use of flow charts also allows multiple participants to review the entire process, ask "what if" questions, and develop alternatives that may be more efficient and effective in providing the services. An example of a flow chart to analyze a process is shown in Figure 13.2.

Figure 13.2 details the steps in process change management. It is critical to identify the problems with a process. These problems are associated with reasons why customers are not satisfied with the product or the service. It is a way of knowing what customer needs and how such needs can be accommodated through design. Design requirements should therefore, match customer needs. A prototype is developed, evaluated, test-piloted to address "what if" questions that may appear in the process. These issues need to be settled before the process is fully implemented. It is essential that existing process must continue to meet the needs of the customer and such processes will, therefore, be considered to be stable and capable. When a process is meeting the needs of the customer, it can benefit from continuous improvement. However, when the process is incapable of meeting such needs, no amount of continuous improvement will restore it to satisfy customer needs. At that stage, it is important to overhaul the process by introducing a new process. Once the new process is introduced, this cycle of continuous improvement-to-reengineering will continue (see Figure 13.2).

Continuous Improvement Versus Breakthrough Thinking

A capable process will be able to meet design requirements and satisfy customer needs. A process can benefit from continuous improvement or

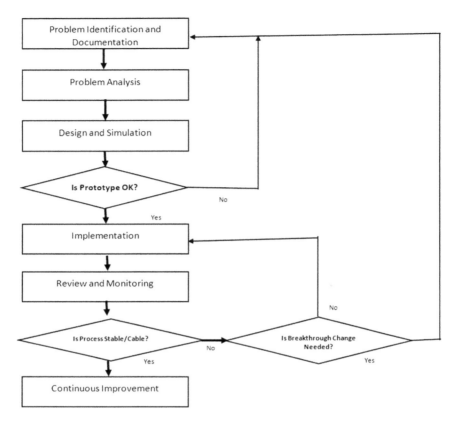

Figure 13.2.   Steps in process change.

breakthrough thinking. A process that can benefit from small incremental improvements overtime can continuously meet the needs of the customer. In other words, small modifications of the process may be sufficient to satisfy the needs of the customer. However, with the rapid proliferation of new technologies and the increasing demands of customers, stringent standards are now imposed on products and services. Thus, when an incremental improvement is no longer enough to meet design specifications, there may a need to completely overhaul the process. This will require dumping the existing process to opt for a new process that will meet the new standards. This is the breakthrough thinking or reengineering. It is important that the new process takes into consideration the human factor issues involved in managing processes. Just as we discussed above, there are threats and anxieties involved when new processes are introduced. As a result, the people should be carried along from the process initiation stage and they should own the process to ensure its successful implementation. A new process today can become obsolete tomorrow. So, it is essential that the process is continuously monitored to know when it is deviating from expected standards, and appropriate action on either continuous improvement or reengineering should be taken to restore the process's operations to standard. Thus, a new process can go through a phase of continuous improvement followed by breakthrough improvement and then continuous improvement (Harrington, 1991).

Tenner and Detoro (1997) used internal process rating to measure efficiency and customer satisfaction rating to measure effectiveness. This helps a business to competitively position itself. Efficiency deals with doing things right while effectiveness is about doing the right things. An inefficient process may operate within its limits and be doing things right without necessarily doing the right things. The right things are those things that will enrich customer experience and therefore, satisfy customer needs. Conversely, in doing the right things, it is important that they are done right and by doing them right, we can optimize the use of resources. Thus, efficiency and effectiveness are crucial in quality function deployment. It is not possible to satisfy customer needs through design without being efficient and effective. The processes that are used to deliver the services to the customer must, therefore, be managed to be both efficient and effective.

Management of Change

People will naturally, resist change especially when they are not carried along. There are anxieties when change is introduced and such anxieties question the person's involvement in the organization. When new processes are introduced to improve efficiency and effectiveness, they are not easily accepted. It is therefore important to pay attention to some of the factors that may impede the new process. That way, change can be managed effectively. Change management here involves the ability to adapt to the new process. Without adaptation to the new process, customer requirements will not be satisfied even when the design requirements are known and matched to meet such requirements. Managing change requires that the organization understands the concern of the people affected by change, devote the necessary resources, communicate effectively, and explain unambiguously, the need for process change.

We have mentioned the two major process initiatives as either continuous improvement or reengineering. Processes that are capable can benefit from incremental changes over time. Such changes are usually not drastic and are easier to adapt to. However, when an initiative involves reengineering, a completely new process is introduced and this may create a lot of anxiety and pain that must be managed effectively otherwise, such initiative may fail. Some of the reasons for failure are:

- The people are not carried along in the planning process. All those that are affected by the process or are active participants should be involved in the planning process to appreciate the reason for process change. They need to begin early to fit themselves into the new process and see how they can adapt to achieve the organizational goal.

- It is important to know where the process is today and the future state that is expected and why. New processes are often introduced to satisfy customer needs and achieve competitiveness. Without the ability to meet customer needs, the business will not survive. Using this as a premise will help to garner support for the new process and achieve active participation of key stakeholders in achieving successful implementation of the process.

- There has to be a structured approach to address the people-oriented issues. For example, there should be opportunities for training and retraining to adapt to the new process. There should also be a concerted effort to understand the personal differences that may have been affected by both organizational history and culture. Efforts should therefore be made to develop different approaches of working with people to get their buy-in.

- Organizational resources must be committed to successfully implement new processes. This will require top management involvement and support. When top management is committed to change, other members of the organization will follow. The support of top management can influence other organizational structures and provide the needed resources to implement change. The role of top management is essential in committing both financial resources and time and also in ensuring that the need for process change is disseminated effectively. Top management encourages and empowers all to take the risks to manage change. When top management is committed, some of the structures that may hamper process change can gradually be broken down and people will see that there is a systematic effort to introduce change to achieve organizational goals and objectives.

- Even with all the best efforts, there may still be some resistance to change. This should always be expected. However, it is important to create opportunities for people to express their fears and resistance to process change. Their unique positions should be understood and their fears should be honestly and truthfully addressed to build their trust and support.

IDENTIFYING, ANALYZING, AND IMPLEMENTING A PROCESS

The steps for identifying, analyzing, and implementing a process to satisfy customer needs are outlined below. These steps are not static. They can be adapted to solve different process problems.

Process Identification

1. Define your job roles, responsibilities, and expectations.
2. What processes are needed to achieve your job roles and expectations?
3. Map out the process showing the steps that are involved.
4. Identify the stakeholders.
5. Identify the outcomes of the process, and the values created.
6. What performance measures are used? And how long does it take to complete the process? Prioritize the processes and select the most important process for study.
7. What resources do you need to complete the process?
8. How does the process compare with that of the competitor?
9. Which competitor is considered to be the best in class and why?
10. Identify the strengths, weaknesses, opportunities, and threats. Can any of these be harnessed to improve the process?
11. Can the process benefit from continuous improvement or does it need breakthrough thinking?
12. Do you have the resources to be best in class?

Process Analysis

1. Develop a flow chart of the process
2. Develop a cross-functional team to include all the key stakeholders.
3. Organize team meetings not lasting more than 1 hour to review the flow chart and develop a comprehensive flow chart.
4. Work with the team for the subsequent steps that follow.
5. Review the process to identify potential bottlenecks and redundancies.

6. Can the process be streamlined by removing redundant steps and bottlenecks?
7. If the process can be streamlined, re-map the process to show a new flow chart.
8. Compare the redesigned flow chart to the current process and outline your expectations.
9. Conduct a test run of the new process with a small sample set.
10. Collect data, validate the data, and verify the data by comparing process performance using established performance measures (Note: You must have comparable data on the results generated by the current process).
11. How long does this process take in comparison to the current process? What is the cost?
12. Is the proposed process robust enough? Are there alternative processes and how do they compare?
13. How does this process compare to benchmark processes? Can it be further improved on?

Process Implementation

1. Once the process has been validated and verified and technical hitches taken out, it is ready for implementation.
2. What is the reaction of the employees to the new process? Is there enough "buy-in?"
3. Are the employees trained and made aware of the implementation stages?
4. Is there a plan for phased implementation? And where will the implementation first start? Aim to get a good support and achieve good results or home run. This would encourage further implementation.
5. Continue to study, obtain feedback, improve, and expand implementation.
6. Track and monitor the process to determine "outliers" and when the process may be due either for continuous improvement or for reengineering.
7. Always align the process to the strategic thinking of the organization and continue to focus on efficiency and effectiveness.

Business Process Reengineering at Porsche Research and Development Center

Porshe AG's is a successful example of reengineering application. Reengineering was introduced to reduce the running time of part procurement from 30 days to 1 day. This requires that the construction time should be about 20 hours. This was achieved after running the prototype for 20 weeks. Several success factors were recorded and are attributed to the establishment of effective team and online process control supported by IT implementation (Zinser, Baumgartner, & Walliser, 1998).

CONCLUSION

Process capability is crucial in satisfying customer requirements. A capable process is a stable one and will be able to meet the needs of the customer. A capable process can benefit from incremental improvement overtime. However, overtime, the process may not be able to meet the established standards and irrespective of continuous improvement, it will still not be capable. Thus, reengineering of the process will be required. We have also discussed the need for process mapping to identify all the activities that are involved in a process and to streamline the process by removing redundant activities and bottlenecks. The steps to achieve process improvement were also identified.

REFERENCES

Fisher J. M. (n.d.). The process of transition. Retrieved December 16, 2018, from http://www.businessballs.com

Harrington, H. J. (1991). *Business process improvement: The breakthrough strategy for total quality, productivity, and competitiveness*. New York, NY: McGraw Hill.

Tenner, A. R., & DeToro, I. J. (1997). *Process redesign: The implementation guide for managers*. Reading, MA: Addison-Wesley.

Zinser, S., Baumgärtner, A., & Walliser, F.-S. (1998). Best practice in reengineering: a successful example of the Porsche research and development center. *Business Process Management Journal, 4*(2), 154–167, https://doi.org/10.1108/14637159810212325

ABOUT THE AUTHOR

Christian N. Madu is professor of management science at Pace University, New York and the SPDC JV Professor of Environmental Management and Control at the University of Nigeria. He is the author of more than 17 books and 150 technical papers in leading academic journals in the areas of management science, quality management, and environmental management. His recent books include the *Handbook of Disaster Risk Reduction & Management*(2017) and *Handbook of Sustainability Management* published in 2012. Professor Madu's publications have appeared in leading academic journals such as *Energy Policy, Land Use Policy, Journal of Environmental Management, Journal of Cleaner Production, Sustainable Cities and Society, Expert Systems with Applications, Technological Forecasting & Social Change, Decision Sciences, Journal of Operational Research Society, Mathematical and Computer Modeling, Computers & Operations Research, European Journal of Operations Research, Computers & Industrial Engineering, Applied Mathematics Letters, IIE Transactions, Long Range Planning, Socio-economic Planning Sciences*, and so forth. Professor Madu has consulted for several international organizations. He is a Fellow of several professional organizations. He currently serves as the editor-in-chief of *Current Environmental Management* and is on the editorial board of more than 30 journals.

Professor Madu's research work and activities continue to benefit from the generosity of The Shell Petroleum Development Company of Nigeria Limited (SPDC) who endowed him with the SPDC JV Professorship in Environmental Management and Control. The resources provided by the position continue to make it possible for Professor Madu to expand his research scope in the areas of environmentalmanagement.